THE LLAMA MANIFESTO

VOLUME ONE THE ADVENT

KURT THEOBALD

Copyright © 2010 by Kurt Theobald

All rights reserved, including the right to reproduce this book or portions thereof in any form whatsoever. For information, address Llama Publishing.

Format and Design by Joey Southard

Hardcover ISBN: 978-0-9830032-3-6
Soft cover ISBN: 978-0-9830032-4-3
eBook ISBN: 978-0-9830032-5-0

TABLE OF CONTENTS

INTRODUCTION — vii
SETTING THE STAGE — xi
PREPARING YOUR MIND TO READ THIS BOOK — xvii

PART ONE THE PURSUIT OF HAPPINESS

CHAPTER 1	**CAN'T BUY ME LOVE**	3
CHAPTER 2	**BEING HAPPY VS FEELING HAPPY**	11
CHAPTER 3	**HOW TO BE HAPPY**	15
CHAPTER 4	**DISCOVERING WHO YOU TRULY ARE**	21
CHAPTER 5	**THE PATH MOST TRAVELED BY**	29

PART TWO YOU ARE A LEADER

CHAPTER 6	**ORIGINAL DESIGN**	35
CHAPTER 7	**TURNING SELF INSIDE OUT**	39
CHAPTER 8	**THE HEART**	49
CHAPTER 9	**THE HEAD**	59
CHAPTER 10	**THE BODY**	65

CHAPTER 11	**THREE KEYS TO PRODUCTIVITY**	71
CHAPTER 12	**THE BELLY AND APPETITE**	81
CHAPTER 13	**THE WILL**	93

PART THREE WHAT A LEADER IS

| CHAPTER 14 | **WHAT DOES A LEADER DO?** | 101 |
| CHAPTER 15 | **NATURAL ORDER** | 107 |

EIGHT CORE VIRTUES

CHAPTER 16	**HONESTY**	113
CHAPTER 17	**OPENNESS**	117
CHAPTER 18	**TRANSPARENCY**	125
CHAPTER 19	**PASSION AND DISCIPLINE**	133
CHAPTER 20	**PROACTIVITY**	143
CHAPTER 21	**HUMILITY VS EGO**	151
CHAPTER 22	**THE PATH OF FOOLS**	157
CHAPTER 23	**GRACE**	161

THE THINGS THAT BIND US

CHAPTER 24	**FEAR**	171
CHAPTER 25	**GREED**	177
CHAPTER 26	**LEADERS ARE SELFLESS**	183
CHAPTER 27	**THE NEED FOR CONTROL**	187

PART FOUR **THE JOURNEY**

CHAPTER 28	**WOOING YOUR HEART**	195
CHAPTER 29	**EMBRACING PAIN & DISCOMFORT**	203
CHAPTER 30	**YOUR RELATIONSHIP WITH YOUR SELF**	209
CHAPTER 31	**LEADERS MAKE BIG COMMITMENTS**	213
CHAPTER 32	**LEADERS ARE INFINITELY CREATIVE**	227
CHAPTER 33	**THE RESULTS OF LEADERSHIP**	231
CHAPTER 34	**WHAT LEADERSHIP LOOKS LIKE**	239

THE CYCLE OF GROWTH   243
A CALL TO ACTION   246
ACKNOWLEDGEMENTS   249

INTRODUCTION

In writing this book, I consciously chose to break just about every publishing rule you can imagine. I wrote it in a bubble. Nobody was editing it. Nobody was proofreading it. Nobody was even reading it. I didn't have a clearly predefined audience. I didn't have a predefined marketing plan, much less a publishing deal. And when people asked me who my target market was, I would fumble around for an intelligent-sounding answer to avoid the reality that I had committed marketing suicide by accepting that "this book is for everyone." It was just me writing, reading, and editing this book in my imaginary desert because that's how it was supposed to be. And I think that what has resulted is truly extraordinary.

Shortly after I had completed the initial manuscript of this book, I was reading through it, and something clicked in me, and I thought to myself, "I wrote this book for me." As I read through it, I was being challenged and engaged by it. I found myself having to ask tough questions of myself and sought the answers for days, sometimes weeks. The book hadn't even been published yet, and it was already challenging its first reader: The author.

This is no ordinary book. I don't call it a manifesto lightly. I was compelled by an overwhelming force pressing outward from deep within me, like steam under great pressure, to communicate this to those who would listen, and I have accepted that responsibility. Sharing it with friends, family, and unsuspecting strangers wasn't enough. I had seen too many people positively impacted by it to keep it quiet. So I committed to it with wild abandon.

Still, in my humanity, I must admit I second-guessed myself dozens of times throughout the writing and production process. Was I a fool to write it exactly how I wanted to write it without sensitivity to a particular market segment? Would anyone even read it? If they did read it, would they get it? Would they read the first few chapters and throw it away in disgust or boredom? Would it ruin my reputation and mar my professional life forever?!

As these questions plagued me, a consistent, rebellious voice combated the fear from deep within me, saying, "Screw it! I don't care. *People need to read this book!* I'm not going to be so selfish as to yield to some pathetic fear of public scrutiny and withhold something this important from the world. This is fresh, new, even revolutionary, and people need this to understand their potential in all its greatness!" Admittedly, it was a great pep talk, and ultimately effective.

Truth be told, I don't have any idea if the market is ready for this book. But that doesn't really matter to me. What matters to me is that it benefits you. One thing of which I am unwaveringly confident is the rich value of the content in this book, and I know this because of the impact the truth it contains has had in my life and in the lives of others.

I encourage you to persevere through any objections or confusion you experience along the way because if you persevere to the end, I am certain that the truth in this book can have a powerfully enriching effect on your life. And if you read it a second time a year later, I believe you would experience greater enrichment, and even greater on the third and fourth readings. What is offered is something you "get" over a lifetime, not by reading a single book one time. It is too rich to take it all in at once. I'm consistently learning new things from it and being challenged afresh by it. That's exciting to me, and I'm excited to share it with you. I hope it benefits you even half as much as it has me.

SETTING THE STAGE

My fondest childhood memory is of my father playing "monster" with my three older siblings and me. All of us kids would climb onto the sofa, and he would prowl and growl on all fours on the carpet to create the mood. Then he would start coming towards us, and we would all squeal and yell and laugh in unabated excitement and the "safe fear" you feel with someone you trust. My dad would grab one of us by the ankles and drag us off the couch. The other siblings would attack him to save the stolen child, and we would all wrestle for a bit, and eventually, my dad would relent and be defeated. Then as he lay there defeated, he would suddenly start moving and growling again, and we would all flee back to the sofa for another round. Not surprisingly, my fondest childhood memory is a memory of trust and joy.

My worst childhood memory was a night when my mother and all of us children were watching "Magnificent 7," an old western show. My dad had told my mom we couldn't watch it, so when he saw us watching it all together, it was the straw that broke the camel's back. He tore the TV from the wall and rushed outside with it in fury. With my mother leading the way, we all ran out after him onto the concrete patio. We were furious at him for disrupting our fun. I really don't remember the words that were exchanged as my parents shouted at each other. All I remember is, at the peak of desperation, my father raised the TV above his head and slammed it onto the concrete as hard as he could, shattering it into pieces.

My mom, in tears, picked up a handful of gravel and threw it at him with words of hate. Following her example, all my siblings and I picked up gravel by handfuls and threw them at him as well as he walked away in defeat towards his Volkswagen repair shop at the top of the hill. We had won. We had defeated him, vanquished the enemy with righteous anger and hate. I can't imagine how he must have wept that night, completely abandoned and despised by those closest to him, by his own children. By me.

My father was a visionary. He saw things nobody else saw. Instead of seeing what was, he saw the possibility of what could be. But while he saw many great things, he had difficulty bringing them to pass, and other people were unable to see the value in what he envisioned and created. My mom didn't like his visions. She told him they were useless and that he just needed to focus on fixing broken VWs. In his younger years, my dad stood strong. He saw bigger things and focused on his visions as an extension of who he was. To not pursue such the things he deemed important would have been a betrayal of his strong Heart.

I remember the second most poignant memory of my childhood was when my dad would walk down to the house after a day's work, and my mom would check his front shirt pocket to see if there was a folded check in it. That's where my dad always kept payments from his customers. Every time there was a check in his front pocket, it seemed like my mom would be happy and they would love each other. When there was no check, I could feel the disappointment, regret, and resentment in the air, and I hated it.

I wanted my mom and dad to be happy together, to love each other all the time. So I naturally started to check my dad's front pocket every day after work. There usually wasn't anything, but when there was, I was excited about the day because I knew it would be a good one. I usually got to my dad when he was halfway down the hill, and when I found out he had a check in his front pocket, I remember taking it and running as fast as I could to report the good news to my mom.

My dad became measured by whether or not he had a check in his front pocket. If it was there, it meant he was doing well; if it wasn't, he needed to work harder and focus. I remember taking on my mother's exact same perspective on this and holding my dad accountable to it. I can't imagine how heart-wrenching it must have been to my dad for his worth to be measured by his ability to make money when his Heart wanted so much more; his Heart cared about the visions he had. But nobody else in our family did. We all thought he was crazy, which was further supported by the fact that he took tranquilizers and anti-psychotic drugs throughout most of his adult life. I remember he slept a lot when he was on these drugs, but Mom was happier.

He didn't want to take these drugs, though, because they stymied his creativity and his Passion. They clouded his vision. So he wouldn't take them. Then my parents would fight more. And when it got really bad, my mom would have him admitted to a psych ward. He would come back more complacent, more compliant, and seemingly happier. But this artificial sense of stability only lasted for a few weeks. He inevitably would fall back into his routine and stop taking the drugs that clouded his mind.

If I were in his shoes, I probably would have done the same

thing. A life without vision, Passion, and creativity is certainly not living. I think drugs made him feel like the walking dead. My mom thought she wanted him to be undead. I wanted him to be undead. But my dad, albeit socially awkward and insecure, was an amazing man. He could have made so many people successful in his life and been wildly successful himself as a result. But he didn't, and he wasn't. Quite the contrary. Last time I heard from him, he was homeless in LA by his own choice. After my mom left him for another man, the conflict between my dad's desire for intimate connection with my mother and to be fully true to himself destroyed him. For a year after my mom separated from him, he tried to prove he was worthy of her and capable of being stable. But it was clear that her mind was made up.

I remember my dad trying to act calm and "together" as they filled out divorce documents in my mom's bedroom. I wonder if he felt any relief, or just gut-wrenching anxiety from believing that the two things he wanted most were incompatible: To be fully himself and have an intimate relationship with my mother.

I learned a lot from them. Only now am I starting to learn the good lessons they taught, though. I didn't even realize it, but my mom's belief that my dad's visions and ideas were stupid and crazy supported me in believing that my visions and ideas were stupid and crazy. I think she saw my dad's tendencies in me as a teenager as I skipped from job to job, not really satisfied with anything and always wanting to do something "different," to carve out a path of on my own.

My visions always included building something that didn't exist before, or creating totally new things. But all the while, I had a deep-seated belief that victory wasn't possible, that I was going to fail because my visions were stupid and foolish, just like my dad's.

And what I've realized as I've uncovered this deep realization is that when I betrayed my dad that night when he smashed the TV, I was really betraying myself. I was really throwing rocks at the stupid, crazy visions in my own Heart.

My first business was selling sour gumballs to my classmates in second grade. While walking through a bulk food store, I saw a big container of about 100 sour gumballs for around $10. My creative, entrepreneurial spirit immediately envisioned the business. Sell sour gumballs at school for 25 cents apiece and make a killing. I probably only sold a couple dozen before quitting. I didn't quit because it wasn't working. It was! Like a charm! I quit because I didn't believe it was important. I didn't believe it was worth it. I didn't believe there was an opportunity for any significant victory in it. I chose to fail, and in so doing, I betrayed my Heart again. If I had persisted in that, I fully believe that today I would be a much wealthier and stronger man.

I have found that the challenge has become finding a way to marry my reckless, wild Heart with my doubting, rigid Head. How do I allow my Heart to be free and "crazy" while actually producing results and living abundantly? Without realizing it earlier on, this was the burning question coming from the deep parts of my Soul. As I've consciously sought out the answer, I've been recording my discoveries. This book is the first of what I discovered. It is a guidebook for your journey into leadership.

To be frank, what follows is not enough. It's a good foundation, but I would suggest that you have to *connect to and experience* your whole Self before it becomes real to you, before it becomes truly powerful. I can offer you guidance toward that end, but the choice to take action and transcend into your True Self is yours and yours alone.

PREPARING YOUR MIND TO READ THIS BOOK

Welcome to The Llama Manifesto. If you're a bit lost as to how what I've said so far has anything to do with leadership, that's okay. Just bear with me. I would like to take a moment to welcome you to your journey through this book and to make a few initial suggestions to help you get the most out of it. This is not a one-sided activity. This is a dialogue. It requires action on your part. If I suggest you engage in a particular activity, like asking yourself or someone else a question, do it. Don't stand on the sidelines. This is a journey that you can actually traverse. It helps you not at all if you see the map for a journey without starting or completing it. This book was designed for your engagement. Engage. Walk the journey. Don't just read about it.

One more note. I use all manner of personal vocabulary in this book. Please try not to get hung up on semantics. If I use a word that is strange to you or brings up certain predefined feelings, step out of those feelings and try to understand the spirit of my communication. I am the chief in this blunder, so I know well how quickly it can corrupt a learning opportunity.

This book revolves around a core belief: That you are a

leader. Consider your internal dialogue when I tell you that: You are a leader. What feedback do you get from yourself? "This book isn't for me then." "I couldn't lead." "Yes I am!" "I'm scared of leading." "Some people are leaders; others are followers."

As you read, note your internal feedback as I make suggestions and as I present foreign concepts to you. You can choose not to accept or even engage in particular suggestions or ideas, but note what internal dialogue caused you to shrink back from it. This alone can teach you much about yourself.

Leadership has always been a focal point at Classy Llama Studios, after which this book is named. Being a Llama means being a true and strong leader. That's our culture and has been from the beginning. But as we progress, we learn more about leadership, and it continues to be an intense challenge. We, as individuals and as a team, are perpetually a work in progress.

I will not start by talking about you as a leader, but rather, I will lay the foundation for why you are a leader, why it matters that you are a leader, and why it would be very worthwhile to you and the rest of the world for you to step into that aspect of who you are.

One final note before we jump in. As you read, take what you will and leave the rest. I'm not trying to impose my perspective on you, nor am I asking you to agree with everything I say. I am merely presenting my perspective up as an offering to you. What you do with it is your choice.

THE LLAMA MANIFESTO
— ON ONE PAGE —

PURSUIT OF HAPPINESS

- WHAT YOU REALLY WANT IS TO BE HAPPY.
- YOU CAN'T BUY HAPPINESS.
- FEELING HAPPY DOES NOT EQUAL BEING HAPPY.
- BEING HAPPY IS ACHIEVED BY ALIGNING WITH YOUR PURPOSE, IDENTITY, AND ORIGIN.

YOU ARE A LEADER

- YOU ARE A LEADER. IT'S PART OF YOUR IDENTITY.
- LEADERSHIP STARTS WITH AND REVOLVES AROUND THE LEADERSHIP OF SELF.
- YOU MUST UNDERSTAND YOUR **SELF** TO LEAD YOUR **SELF** EFFECTIVELY.

WHAT A LEADER IS

- LEADERSHIP REVOLVES AROUND GROWING, BEING CREATIVE, AND SERVING OTHERS.
- LEADERS OF SELF ARE OPEN, HONEST, TRANSPARENT, PASSIONATE, DISCIPLINED, PROACTIVE, HUMBLE, AND GRACIOUS.
- LEADERS OPPOSE GREED'S INFLUENCE.
- LEADERS DO NOT NEED CONTROL.
- LEADERS EMBRACE PAIN AND DISCOMFORT.

THE JOURNEY OF LEADERSHIP

- LEADERS DEVELOP A STRONG RELATIONSHIP WITH THEIR SELVES.
- LEADERS LEAD A LIFE OF NEVER-ENDING ADVENTURE AND CREATIVITY, DRIVEN BY STRONG COMMITMENTS.
- LEADERS PLAY FOR A LIVING. THEY PLAY ALL IN, ALL THE TIME.
- LEADERS BEAR MUCH FRUIT AND MULTIPLY.

PART ONE
THE PURSUIT OF HAPPINESS

CHAPTER ONE

CAN'T BUY ME LOVE

WHAT YOU REALLY WANT IS TO BE HAPPY.

The Llama Manifesto begins with a very appropriate question, a question that I frequently ask early on in my interviewing process, a process that my team has affectionately named the "gruelfest" because it is notoriously challenging. The question is: "What do you want?" I've received all manner of answers to that question, but what I have found consistently is that, deep down, people just want to be happy. Unfortunately, we as a society have a really messed up idea of what it takes to be happy. We are all confused, at least in practice, at some level on the matter. I'm not trying to demean you by saying this; I speak from my own experience as I'm a perpetual student that constantly finds new ways in which I have misunderstood the meaning and path to happiness, and I am confident I will continue to make new and similar discoveries. I want to offer you what enlightenment I can on the matter of happiness and provide a fundamental blueprint for its pursuit and acquisition, all under the clear understanding that I have not arrived and strive to practice what I preach on a daily basis, some days more successfully than others.

At one point in my life, my brain operated programmatically, and by that I mean that society had taught me to think a certain way, and I had fallen in rank and file. I believed that a cutthroat, take-as-much-as-I-can, get-the-job-done, I'll-fake-it-'til-I-make-it attitude was the most expedient path to happiness, and I was bullheadedly committed to make it work. But then I stumbled upon a realization that changed my life forever. I discovered that Adam Smith, acknowledged as the father of modern capitalism, while providing tons of amazing insights into capitalistic economy, was fundamentally wrong in his 1776 economic treatise *Wealth of Nations*. Smith was trying to answer a question: "What is the most effective and efficient way to meet market demand?" He concluded that the answer was for everyone to pursue their own interests, represented by goods and services, or "stuff," as I call it. What he failed to recognize is that the market ultimately demands happiness, not stuff.

The problem with Smith's theory is that it is based on the belief that the purpose of the supply market is to produce stuff that people demand. This perspective is superficial. "The Market" is just people, and the reason people demand goods and services is because they desire or "demand" happiness. Unfortunately, the market is easily persuaded to believe that goods and services can make them happy, when in truth, happiness is not achieved from anything that people can obtain outside of themselves. But this theory still managed to persuade me as well as gain pandemic traction over the past 250 years for a reason quite separate from Truth.

Think about it. Smith's theory gives everyone a very convenient excuse, a justification, to serve Self. We humans look for any excuse to do what is easiest, and Adam Smith gave a very cogent dissertation on how beneficial it is to be egocentric. That doesn't make it true or good or effective. It just makes it convenient.

Consider what applying Smithsonian economics has produced over the past couple of centuries. There has been an increase in total goods and services produced, but quality of life has stagnated or declined. Ask people what their life purpose is nowadays, and you'll more often than not get a blank stare or an uncertain, inauthentic answer.

YOU CAN'T BUY HAPPINESS.

Step out of your box for a moment and consider that money isn't actually what you want. You want to be happy. It appears that those who have money are more often happy than those who do not, which is why we pursue money, thinking that it is at least a foundational key to happiness. But have you ever considered that those who are happy and wealthy achieved their wealth as a byproduct of their happiness rather than their happiness being a byproduct of their wealth? We know that wealth can't buy Happiness, and yet it seems so closely tied to it! I believe that many people become wealthy because they step into who they really are, and that step, which is already producing happiness in their lives, produces wealth over time. The same focus that made them happy also makes them wealthy. Wouldn't that be amazing?

When the Llama team started working together, money was never the goal. We wanted to produce extraordinary results in service to others. That was and still is our priority. Starting in April of 2008, after six months of trying to sustain the office we were in from a previous business venture, we worked out of my garage for 18 months while we gained traction. Thankfully, it was a two-car garage, but by the time we had 10 people in there, it didn't feel like it. We literally had to move our chairs out of the way any time someone needed to leave the garage. Times were scarce, but we were in it for a cause, not comfort, so it didn't matter. This created a culture of personal investment, in which team members asked how they could be doing more for our clients, for each other, and for the business, and the only discussion of money was in context of growing our capacity to serve or covering base level needs. Being a Llama was never about being selfish. From the very beginning, it was a commitment to our joint mission and vision. And that's what kept us going in the early days.

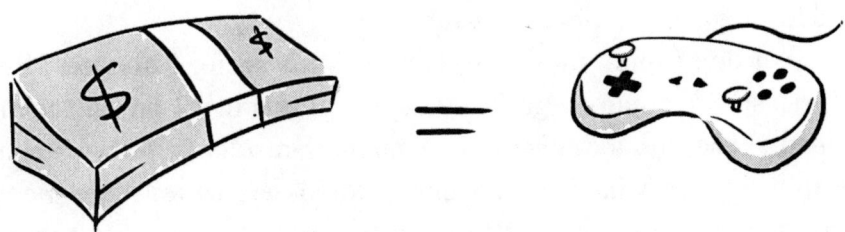

MONEY EQUALS CONTROL   *Fig. 1.1*

Unfortunately, money has become the primary cause for organized effort, but as cliché as it sounds, money cannot buy happiness; it can only buy Stuff, and somehow many people have become deceived into thinking that Stuff will make them happy because the almighty ad says it will. Money buys one core commodity: Control *(see Fig 1.1)*. Whether it's control over goods, other people's time, a plot of land, a ship, a package of snack crackers, it's all control. The majority of people have been deceived to think that control is critical to acquiring happiness because control gets them comfort, pleasure, and security, and money is their medium for acquiring these things. I'm certainly not suggesting there is anything wrong with control. Control is a tool that can be used for good or evil. But it is not synonymous with happiness.

That's not the only damage that Smithsonian economics causes. It also creates an environment of human commoditization, which just means that people look at other people as commodities, valued only according to their relative usefulness. Consider that we use primarily economic metaphors when discussing relationships: "We *invest* in relationships." "We *value* our friends." "We have a *human resources* department." "We're trying to increase *intellectual capital*." "They're a real *asset* to the team." And on and on. We don't view people as people but as objects that we can utilize and leverage to get what we want.

I don't think most people notice this societal disease. But there's still one more significant aspect to this that I haven't mentioned. The commoditization of humans results in transactional relationship, in which we do things for others as an investment, expecting a return for the effort and resources invested. In Smithsonian economics, you only do something for someone else if you see greater benefit than cost to yourself as a result. It's still totally hinging on what is in Self's best interest.

Ultimately, what Smithsonian economics promotes is the supremacy of Egocentrism, the prioritization of Self at any cost to others. Ego is the reason we commoditize others and conduct relationships transactionally, and Ego has three children: Greed (we believe that acquiring our material wants will make us happy), Fear (we believe that security and stability will make us happy), and Ignorance (we believe that comfort and ease will make us happy). Smithsonian economics and the leadership that grows out of it is built on these three elements, and they result in catastrophic failure, failure to deliver the market's primary demand for happiness.

My Parents Taught Me Everything I Believe About Money

I grew up in an environment where money was the crux point of all conflict. It was the fight. It was something there was never quite enough of. It was how my mom measured my father, which is why I checked his front pocket after his workday. I knew if there was a check, we would have a good evening as a family. If there was no check, all bets were off, and I felt insecure.

There was also a root level judgment fostered in my house that the rich were evil and greedy, having no care for the misfortunate and even when they had the appearance of care, ulterior motives were identified. I despised the rich. I hated that they were not willing to share. I expected they had some cheesy excuse for not sharing like that people needed to "earn their due."

And yet, I very much wanted to be a rich person. I didn't want my family to struggle like my parents did. Unfortunately, at a deep level, I had learned to associate conflict, inadequacy, greediness, evil, and a lack of integrity with money. With so many associations, for years, I subconsciously sabotaged my attempts at producing any level of prosperity. I realized more recently that I was so afraid of money's negative implications that I wrote it off as "unimportant" and "not that valuable." My awareness of these subconscious beliefs about money set me on a path that leads to financial prosperity. That is not to contradict the reality that money does not equal happiness, but it is often an important participant in the pursuit of happiness.

Right now, I would like to offer you the same opportunity to look behind you and see what experiences have shaped your perspective on money. Look at the financial results you've produced and realize that you've created those results. They haven't happened to you. Do you hoard money? Do you despise and hate it? Do you have a "do-whatever-it-takes-to-get-it" mentality? If you won the lottery, would you feel like you had arrived? What did money represent in your home? I think that most of you will come to realize the same thing I did: Scarcity controls me. I continue to struggle with an "either-or" mentality. Instead of asking questions of how I can have both of two seemingly competing interests, I just ask, "Which one will I give up?" This applies to money, time, and all other resources. If you hear yourself saying "I don't have the time," or "I can't afford it," I would suggest you're living from a limited, scarce economy at that moment, and I believe there is a different choice.

I remember feeling alone and desperate in my pursuit of happiness. I defaulted to pursuing fame and fortune. That is what society was telling me would give me happiness: Everything I watched on TV, everything I learned in school, everything my parents had taught me. I thought I wasn't happy because I didn't have money. That was my paradigm.

Eventually, I learned that life is about being happy while money can only make you feel happy. And yes, there is a huge difference; so huge, in fact, it's worth an entire chapter…

CHAPTER TWO

BEING HAPPY VS FEELING HAPPY

FEELING HAPPY DOES NOT EQUAL BEING HAPPY.

The natural next step is to define what it takes for you to be happy. Before moving forward, however, I want to make absolutely clear that "being happy" is fundamentally different from "feeling happy," and people often get these two confused. Feeling happy is merely feeling pleasant emotions, which is great in the appropriate context, but not every context. A person might utterly hate themselves and utterly hate being alive, which certainly is not being happy, but because they inject heroin into their eyeballs or go to the movies or eat fast food, they "feel happy." If you are not truly happy, and you use external activities to make you feel happy, the activities are merely pain-killing medication. If you're not really happy, the last thing you need is to feel happy. Pain occurs as a result of stress, which occur when things are not in alignment or unity. If you don't feel the pain that accompanies unhappiness, you lack an essential ingredient in facing the things that are keeping you from being happy.

Gold is refined and purified by placing it over heat and churning it. As the gold churns, imperfections come to the surface and can then be removed. In the same way, your life can be in a constant state of refinement and purification. Friction causes heat, and heat will start the churning process to get things moving in the right direction, bringing issues to the surface that you can then resolve as they are in plain view. You can't know about them until the refining process takes its course. On the other hand, trying to keep your life frictionless, cold, and static will keep the imperfections hidden until the stresses of life boil over and they can be hidden no longer. Eventually, your ugly interior will be exposed, or it will create disease within you and kill you. Would you rather be proactively leading the process of refinement within yourself or futilely trying to fight against it? It's crazy, but the three things we absolutely must have for extraordinary personal growth are the three things we often avoid at all costs: Friction, Tension, and Pressure.

Friction, Tension, and Pressure are forms of stress. Purging is the act of applying stress in order that the good stuff remains while the bad stuff gets pushed out or destroyed. The goal of the purging process is to remove all of the junk. A large portion of that junk is institutions of obfuscation and opacity, those modes of operation and systems that have been put in place to keep everyone around us in the dark about the ugliness within us. Enron always comes to mind when I think of this. Everything seemed fine until the final days because they had effectively hidden the whole tangled mess.

Are you an Enron? Is your marriage an Enron? Is your business an Enron? Does everything seem fine, but implosion is imminent?

It is an invasive, uprooting, overwhelming process that removes the cancer within you by force and leaves the good standing. There is often no targeting or focused pressure at first. You simply start by implementing good practices, and the targets come out of hiding and present themselves, at which point they can be surgically removed.

Once you have removed the junk, you have the opportunity to fill the space back in with good replacements, or you can fill it back in with more junk. The governing law of purging, however, is that you *will* fill it back in with something, good or bad. If you reactively fill in the void, you'll most likely just fill it back in with the same junk that you're used to. Only if you choose to fill it in proactively, going out of your way to choose something different, something better, will you be able to effectively fill the space with the good replacements that are in alignment with your core objectives.

This purging process applies to both organizational infrastructure and individual infrastructure. Faulty or inefficient systems and processes within an organization can certainly be uprooted and omitted through purging, and I strongly recommend it. Even as it applies to people, though, the purging process applies to both purging teams of those not in alignment with a mutual objective and to purging cancerous misalignment within individuals that keep them from being optimally effective and happy.

This applies to you as well. The internal process you must go through when pursuing who you are will purge you, removing the chaff and leaving the gold. The more you expose to the heat, the more wholly refined you will be as a result. You will be tempted to hide certain things from the fire, but if you choose to act against your natural instinct and hold your hands in the fire, you will find out what you are made of. Do not let go of this truth in your mind. If you find yourself broken and torn asunder by this process, the natural tendency is to blame some external source, like this book or your spouse or your colleagues. But if you are broken down, it is because you have much within you that is burnable, perhaps even to your very foundation. But if it is burnable, let it burn and replace it with something golden and pure. It is a painful process, but one that can transform and transcend you. Yield to it. Step into the fire and find out what you're made of.

I still leave you with what it means to be happy unanswered, which I will remedy in the next chapter. This is where it starts to get very exciting. And very challenging. Are you ready?

CHAPTER THREE

HOW TO BE HAPPY

Fig. 3.1

Happiness is the alignment with whence, who, and why you are, or put differently, alignment with your Origin, Identity, and Purpose *(Fig 3.1)*. These three fundamental beliefs are also the foundation for your worldview. Basically, how happy you are can be determined by one simple question: What do you believe about your Self?

Have you ever wondered why women stay with men who beat them regularly? It's because of how they answer the question. They tell themselves "I am trash," or "I am worthless," or "I deserve to be abused." All of these statements indicate what they believe about themselves. And because they believe they deserve it, the abuse is, in some respects, welcome and even relieving.

This core belief system affects every aspect of your life. It determines who your friends are, how you treat them, if you want to have children, how hard you work and why you work, and all other actions and decisions you make. In many respects, it is your autopilot mechanism: Why you do what you do without thought or effort. We all have aspects in which we are on autopilot, and each of them can be traced back to how we answer the three fundamental questions of worldview: Why, Who, and Whence you are.

One of the Llamas recently came face-to-face with a belief he held about himself that he felt like he wasn't good enough to do things well. This was during an inquiry about a lack of quality in his work. When problems arise in Llama culture, we don't seek to force performance back on track; we dig. We want to understand why and deal with the root issue rather than just "getting him to do better." Rarely are shortcomings merely skill deficiencies. Unless you're learning something for the first time, there's always a root-level reason you haven't been able to become proficient or why you aren't performing from your proficiency. Whether it's related to your actual Design or what you believe about yourself, there's always a deeper root.

If you ever experience a behavior or an internal block you do not understand, whether your own or another's, look for the fundamental beliefs about Self underlying that behavior. It's there. You'll just have to dig for it. Conduct your own experiments with this theory. I posit that you can source the cause for any choice you make in any circumstance to what you believe about your Origin, Identity, and Purpose.

Before you begin experimenting, though, there is one more fundamental you need to understand. These three core constituents of your worldview and belief system are not created equal. They are a series of questions that must be asked in the right order. Why you are, your Purpose, is begotten by who you are, your Identity; who you are is begotten by whence you are, your Origin. Or put slightly differently, Origin begets Identity; Identity begets Purpose.

Maslow hit the nail on the head in identifying our highest form of existence: Self-actualization. Maslow's definition of self-actualization is ephemeral and poorly founded, so I am bastardizing the term and making it my own.

My version of self-actualization is simply being who you really are: When your actions are a natural extension of who you are. Not who you believe you are, but who you *really* are.

Purpose flows from who you really are, your Identity, and Identity flows from Origin. Discover your Origin, and connect to it; without it, you do not truly know yourself. Then discover your Identity as a result, and your Purpose as a result of that. Then pursue your Purpose with all your Heart in the full knowledge that you are fulfilling who you are as an extension of your Origin. That is the highest form of life and the greatest experience of Fulfillment and Happiness. Did I just solve the meaning of life? No. But I did just give you the building blocks to solve it yourself.

Identity in Reverse

Most people get this backward. They believe that who they are is defined by what they do rather than what they do being a result of who they are. They say "I do; therefore I am," instead of "I am; therefore I do." They derive their identity from their external environment and make choices accordingly rather than their choices flowing from their Identity therefore changing and influencing their external environment. The difficulty is that it is necessary to have an Identity in the first place and to know what it is in order to know what actions are and are not in agreement with it. Nowadays, people largely believe they define their own identities and that what they do defines who they are. The fundamental flaw in this approach of self-identification is that it is entirely subjective, and Truth is, by nature, objective. In other words, you cannot give yourself a true Identity. It's not possible. Even if all the people in the world agreed with your self-identification, it wouldn't make it any truer. You have no authority to give yourself a true Identity, nor can other humans give you a true Identity. Not your parents, not your friends, not your pastor, not your spouse. Nobody. You can only discover Truth; you cannot create it.

Who you really are, your Identity, flows from your Origin. If you are a product of Chance, as so many believe, you have no identity. But even more fall into the camp of "I'm not sure where I come from." If that's your answer to the question, I would suggest that you don't really know who or why you are. If you think you do, you have the cart before the horse. You cannot know who you are if you don't know whence you are. That's like the knife who doesn't know from whence it exists trying to tell the world it's a spoon used for scooping. The creator of the knife, not the knife, is the one who defines who and for what purpose the knife is.

And so Step One on the road to Self-Actualization and the root of being happy is…

CHAPTER FOUR

DISCOVERING WHO YOU TRULY ARE

When I first learned that life was not about fighting for my worth through performance, I was overjoyed. To live from a good Identity that already existed within me meant that I didn't have to fight to be good enough. I already was good enough. Instead, my life became about living from that innate Identity rather than from the falsehoods I had come to believe about myself and the world around me. It was an important point at which I realized my fight was not with the world around me but with the vast world within me.

I was spending so much energy trying to meet the world's demands and expectations for who I ought to be. I wore business suits because it was "the thing to do." I used big words because it made other people approve of me. I used my humor to gain approval; I used my musical talent to gain approval; I used my athleticism to gain approval. Because I didn't connect with the reality that my Identity was "pre-approved" by my Origin, I was desperately fighting for the outside world to validate my adequacy, but it was never enough. I would achieve, achieve, achieve, but the nagging doubt would still be present and lurking.

In the process of building this image to obtain other people's approval, I found I was actually creating more distance between me and the world as my negative beliefs about myself became more and more disparate from the false image I was maintaining to win approval. I became lonely and found myself frequently falling into depression. Everybody else thought I had it together, and that made me even lonelier. I couldn't share the truth about how I felt because that would destroy the image I had worked so hard to create, or just as bad, people would distrust the authenticity of my transparency as feigned modesty and despise me in their Hearts.

The image I had created became my prison. I couldn't escape it. I was damned if I did; damned if I didn't.

My ultimate freedom came through understanding that I didn't need the false image to be approved as worthy and acceptable. I was accepted and approved by my Origin. I was free to be exactly the person I was designed to be, and not only would that be okay, it would produce extraordinarily powerful results. And the more I learned about my Original Design, the more I loved my Self and the less I felt the need for approval from the outside world. I had what I needed already, so I could focus on living out of my Original Design instead of faking it to get approval from others. It was and continues to be a fundamentally important liberation for me.

That being said, I just recently discovered an entirely new area of my life where I have been addicted to approval, so I would suggest you plan to experience a ceaseless series of liberations. There always seems to be another layer to cut through. And when you're finished with one onion, there's always another one sitting right beside it. That's the exciting beauty of growing; there is no end to the potential. The adventure is never over.

The Question

Okay. I want to give you the opportunity to actively engage in this. Ask yourself The Question: "What do I believe about myself right now?" ... Don't just keep reading. Stop. And answer The Question. It happens to be the single most important question you can ask and answer. And might I suggest you answer it from a deep place. Don't go to your intellectual file cabinet and pull out the "Right Answers" folder. Dig deep and be gut-level honest with yourself. You get to decide how valuable this exercise will be for you.

I'm leaving this space here to represent the 3-5 minutes you just paused to introspect and answer the question.

I have asked this question to many, many people, and the internal reaction they experience to The Question varies widely. Some people answer from their intellectual file cabinet, delivering a quick and sharp reply. Others grapple with The Question, their Head's quick response being challenged by something deeper. And many others are simply so out of touch with themselves, they can't answer. I posit that there are up to three members within you that answer The Question: Your Head, your Heart, and your Spirit.

Let me give you a tour of how I believe your Self is structured. When faced with a question about your Self, your Head is typically the first to answer. "I am a lawyer." "I am a Christian." "I am good at drawing." We commonly draw things from the external like what we do or what we enjoy or what we're good at, or use words that embody abstract notions like "Christian," "realist," or "patriot." Whatever our Head responds, I will summarize it by saying it is what we *think* we believe about ourselves.

So let's travel deeper within you. Your Heart is constantly answering The Question, though you might not hear it. In fact, most of the time, you probably don't. But how the Heart answers is critically important because it will tell you what you really believe about yourself. Men are especially terrible at listening to their Hearts because we are afraid of weakness, and the Heart certainly contains many reflections of weakness that we would rather avoid than acknowledge. Women are typically more actively aware of what their Hearts are telling them, which simply gives them more urge to hide what it says. The truth is, typically, both men and women spend a great deal of time hiding or fighting what their Heart is telling them.

What does your Heart tell you? In an unaided environment, the Heart actually has very negative things to say about you. In other words, in an unaided environment, your true self-image is very negative. "I'm a loser." "I'm not good enough." "I'm a fool." "I'm ugly." "I'm worthless." "I'm weak." "I'm a quitter." "I deserve to be punished." "I am helplessly inadequate." "I'm unimportant." "I'm alone."

Why is the Heart so ready to dish out negativity? Good question, which leads us to take a step to the innermost layer of your being: Your Spirit. The Spirit is buried so deeply within you that many people don't even believe it exists. It is hidden beneath all of your emotional, sentimental, conditional, Heart-based layers, which are hidden beneath all of your logical, rational, conditional,

Head-based layers. In other words, you have to dig and dig and dig to find your Spirit, especially if you're older and have had more time to accrue deep layers in your Head and Heart.

Before opening the door to your Spirit, let me first prepare you with an understanding of what it is and how it functions. In the most generic terms, your Spirit is your connection to your Origin, your Creator, or your god. If you do not believe that a god or higher power is your Origin, then you have some serious problems to deal with, not the least of which is your lack of true Identity and Purpose. There is only one true Origin. I believe the one true Origin is יהוה*. But who or what you believe that Origin is makes no difference to the perspective I have to offer about the nature of your Spirit.

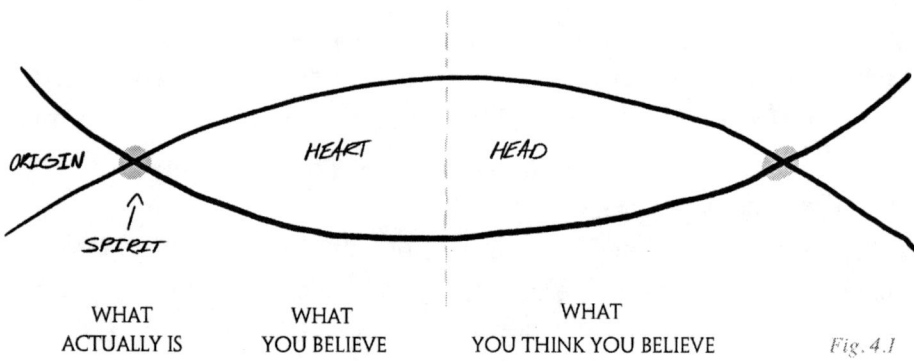

Fig. 4.1

While your Head is the seat of what you *think* you believe about yourself and your Heart is the seat of what you *really* believe about yourself, your Spirit is the source of what *is* *(Fig 4.1)*. It is the source of Actuality, of Objective Truth, of your True Definition. If

---

* Poor English translation: Jehovah

you were fully connected and yielding to your Origin, you would be fully aligned with who you are, and therefore, happy. In short, connecting and yielding to your Origin is the path to the deepest happiness.

What I am about to share is the most challenging idea in this entire book, so if you can stick with me through it, the rest is downhill. Let's open the door to your Spirit and see what we find.

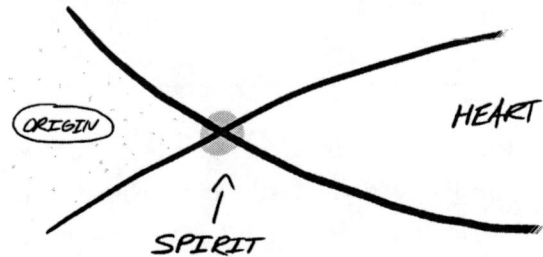

Fig. 4.2

Provided this is your first time opening this door, you may not like what you find: You will find a broken connection, like a lifeline snapped in two and waving wildly in the wind. Your Spirit is disconnected from its Life-Source *(Fig 4.2)*. Like it or not, we are all born into spiritual death, disconnected from our Source of life, our Origin. Or put another way: 100% Original potential; 0% Original kinetic. That's why your Heart is so filled with awful, terrible beliefs about yourself. Instead of having Original Truth flow through it from the inside out, your Heart is taking perspectives from the outside world, and the outside world is filled with falsehood. A very important question to answer is why we are born disconnected, but I will leave that question unanswered so as to maintain focus. But it is a question I strongly recommend you explore and discover.

If you have any hope of being truly happy, your Spirit must

be reconnected to its Source. You are like an electrical appliance, and you need to plug into an electrical outlet that has electricity flowing through it, and you have only one true Origin. Any other perspective is contrary to the very definition of the word "Origin." There are plenty of false outlets that appear to offer what you need, but once you plug into them, you eventually discover they do not. So, how do you get reconnected to your Origin? It's a simple but difficult answer: Seek and ye shall find. It's a process of discovery.

Discovery tip: Seek others who appear to be connected to their Origin and spiritually alive. Ask them for help in your journey of discovery. Don't accept anything at face value. Even people spiritually connected to their Origin have layer upon layer of misunderstanding and falsehood of which they may not even be aware. Be inquisitive and scrutinous.

CHAPTER FIVE

THE PATH MOST TRAVELED BY

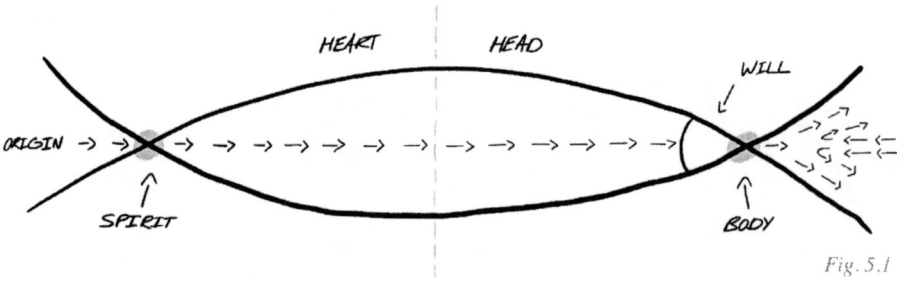

Fig. 5.1

    To aid you in your journey, I will demonstrate and define the internal human structure visually as I understand it. The human structure is intended to be in alignment with the Spirit, allowing Original Design to flow through the human construct and be made manifest in the physical realm *(Figure 5.1)*. The Heart and Head yield perfectly to the Spirit which is connected to Origin, driving choices via your Will, which drive outward actions through your Body that are in perfect alignment with your Origin. In the ordinate structure, as we experience the outside world, that experience flows through us and the Spirit reflects the truth about the outward experience back out of us, maintaining alignment. It works very similarly to a basic input/output system (BIOS) in which the input (our experience of the outside world) is subject to the output (our Spirit's flow).

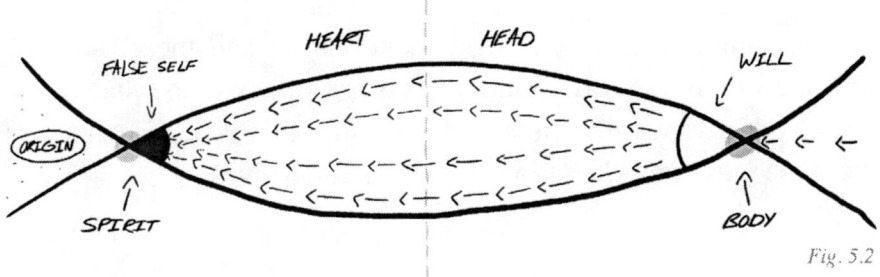

Fig. 5.2

Unfortunately, if the Spirit is disconnected from its Origin, its Lifesource, then there is no output to rule the input *(Fig 5.2)*. The flow is reversed for those whose Spirits are disconnected. If you are not connected to your Origin, you are imprinted from the outside in, your external input defining who you are, your Identity derived from that which comes from without rather than within. This is a false identity, the False Self as I will call it henceforth; it's not really who you are. But at the same time, and this is especially important to note, if who you really are comes from your Origin, and you are disconnected from that, then who you are is undefined, so any jot or tittle of identity derived from the outside world becomes who believe you "really" are, and this falsely derived identity is your False Self. That is why so many secular psychologists believe we are products of our environment, purely reactionary animals. They can see the outside world deeply affecting and shaping inward development. And sadly, these psychologists are right much of the time.

You've probably heard it said many times that children are very "impressionable." I wholeheartedly agree. Our Heart and Head are like soft clay when we are born. And since we are born with Spirits disconnected from our Origin, the clay begins to form reactively to the forces in the physical world. Our parents, teachers, TV, friends, experiences: These shape us. Usually, the longer we are disconnected from our Origin, the harder and more "set" we become in our patterns. Autopilot takes over. We do what we do because it's what we've always done, and we become disconnected from the reasons for the lack of success in our lives.

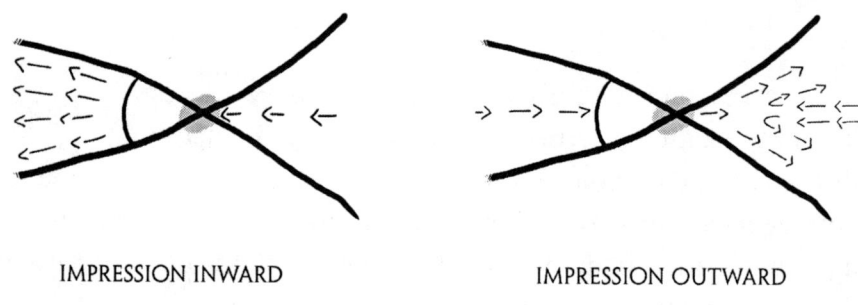

IMPRESSION INWARD   IMPRESSION OUTWARD

Fig. 5.3

Another critical difference to note between spiritual death and life is that people in spiritual death are imprinted upon, they are impressed, sealed by the world's stamp like wax on a letter, whereas people yielding to their Origin act as the stamp, impressing the outside world with Truth and Life *(Figure 5.3)*. Insofar as they yield to their Origin, they are not impressed but impressing, affecting rather than being affected. They create new things and reshape the world around them rather than being shaped. More on this later…

PART TWO
YOU ARE A LEADER

CHAPTER SIX

ORIGINAL DESIGN

What is Your Original Design?

The good news is, I will be sharing many truths about who you were intended to be in this book, not truths derived from the outside world, but Spiritually inspired truths. I expect that how I represent your Original Design will resonate with you. But I will leave that to your judgment. What I have shared with you up to this point is a theory. I will now share with you how that theory practically plays out.

YOU ARE A LEADER. IT'S PART OF YOUR IDENTITY.

Let me start by telling you something you may or may not believe but is true nonetheless: You are a leader. It's part of who you really are. What that means will surprise you, I expect.

Leadership is not always about being at the helm of an organization of people, infrastructure, and resources. It actually starts at a much smaller level than that. It starts with you leading your Self. A leader of Self is one who effectively leads his Body, Head, Heart, and Spirit into alignment with his Origin, becoming more fully himself as he grows. In fact, leadership in its proper role revolves around that pivot point. Leaders of others are responsible to guide and equip others to lead themselves effectively, and leaders of leaders of others are responsible to guide and equip leaders of others to guide and equip others to lead themselves effectively.

LEADERSHIP REVOLVES AROUND GROWING, BEING CREATIVE, AND SERVING OTHERS.

There are an infinite number of concentric levels of leadership. A person could be a leader of leaders of leaders of leaders of leaders of leaders of leaders of leaders of leaders of others. If you enjoy math, I've written a word equation to represent the infinite expansive capacity of leadership:

Leadership (of Leaders)^n of Others = Equipping and guiding others (to equip and guide others)^v to lead themselves.

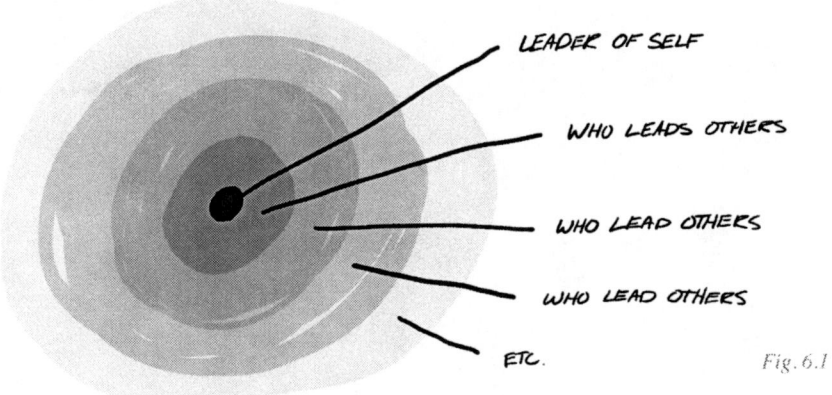

Fig. 6.1

If the equation makes zero sense to you, don't worry about it. The image captures the spirit of the concept just as well *(Fig 6.1)*.

CHAPTER SEVEN

TURNING SELF INSIDE OUT

*YOU MUST UNDERSTAND YOUR **SELF** TO LEAD YOUR **SELF** EFFECTIVELY.*

To lead Self effectively requires that we understand Self. So let's get better acquainted. First, we know the end goal is to be fully aligned with who we really are. But obviously, we need to flesh out what that looks like. Much of your personal Original design is the same as all other humans. In the same way as you are primarily the same physically as other humans, so are you mostly the same metaphysically. We must understand this internal metaphysical structure and specifically how we make decisions through it. As we go along, I will enumerate many other key things we all have in common.

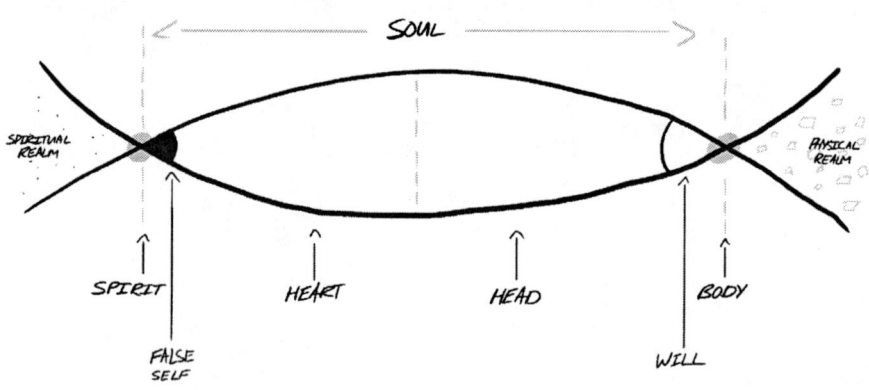

Fig. 7.1

Your Spirit connects you to the spiritual realm, and your Body connects you to the physical realm, or "the world" *(Fig 7.1)*. What is between is what I will call the "Soul," composed of the Heart, Head, derived identity, or False Self, and Will. We are not fully conscious of our entire Soul at all times. Depending on how "in touch" we are with ourselves, our consciousness falls somewhere on the plotted line *(Fig. 7.2)*. Some people are completely out of touch with their Hearts, and if you ask them, "How are you feeling?" they will say, "I don't know," or they will answer from their Heads, saying what they think they feel or ought to be feeling or want you to think they're feeling, because they are not conscious of their feelings. They still feel, but they cannot identify what the feelings are because they are consciously disconnected from their Hearts.

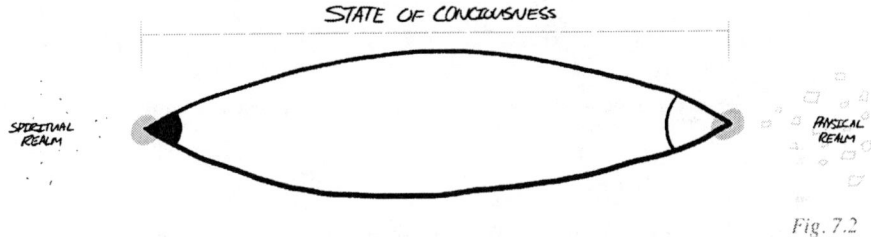

Fig. 7.2

Your state of consciousness varies widely throughout the day. Sometimes, you're fully engaged in a cerebral* endeavor, and you are unconscious of your Heart. That's why many people throw themselves into their work as an escape after a tragedy has occurred, like a death or divorce. By consuming their consciousness with cerebral focus, they avoid consciousness of the hurt in their Heart. I will later explain why this defense tactic cannot and will not work forever.

---

*   Definition: Involving intelligence rather than emotions or instinct.

It is also possible to have moments of spiritual experience when your state of consciousness reaches depths at which very little or nothing is separating you from your Spirit. This rarely or never happens for most people, not because it is impossible, but because they do not know how to consciously travel that deeply within themselves. There are usually many strata of hardened, inaccurate worldviews that get in the way and block access. These must be softened

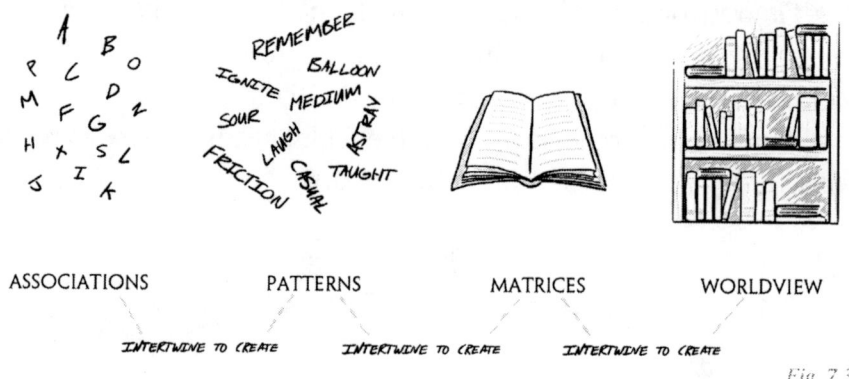

Fig. 7.3

and displaced or removed before such depths can be reached.

At birth, you are structured similarly to a BIOS, a basic input/output system, that draws information from the world around you to develop associations, which intertwine to create patterns, which intertwine to create complex matrices, which intertwine to create fundamental worldviews *(Fig 7.3)*. You don't have much pre-existing software built into you. By and large, you are a blank, reactive slate, just like modern psychology conjectures.

Another important note to understand about the nature of your component parts is that your Heart and Spirit "flow" like water or air or electrical current, and your Head and Body are rigid

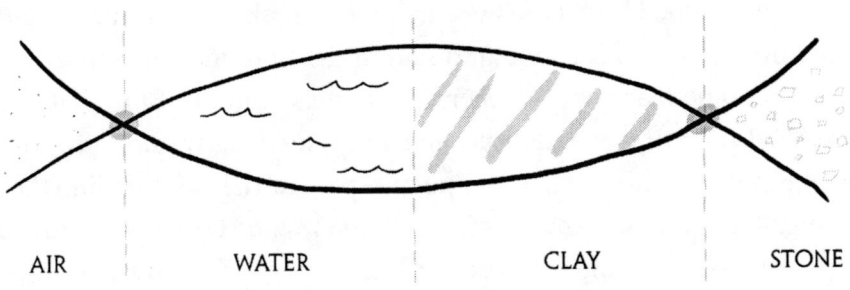

AIR | WATER | CLAY | STONE

Fig. 7.4

structures, like clay and stone vessels that contain the flow in some way *(Fig 7.4)*. In the same way, the spiritual realm is a realm of "flow" whereas the physical realm is "rigid." We are accustomed to being conscious of the "rigid" side of our being, and so it is more comfortable. To mitigate this discomfort, let me first explain the different structural constituents in greater detail before explaining how we make decisions, starting with the Heart.

For many of you reading this, it's probably difficult to even imagine that the spiritual realm exists, or maybe even that your Heart really exists. You're the kind of person that is very careful to qualify everything around you cerebrally because you find that "more dependable." All I can say is that I can totally relate to you. That is my natural bent as well, so for what it's worth, all of this emotional, spiritual stuff weirds me out, too.

Your Heart is the seat of Desire and Passion, which is probably one of the most misunderstood qualities in humanity. Most believe that they are something you either have or have not. While it is true that the Heart is easier for some to feel, and it comes "more naturally" to them, it is not an organ of the Soul that some are born with and others are not. Rather, it is a muscle in our Soul that gets used and strengthens or doesn't and atrophies. Many, through experience, have grown to associate intense pain or risk with feeling their desires and passions and acting upon them and so disconnect from their Hearts, rejecting all Desire as an enemy of survival. Others have become so enraptured with their Desire, they have given up control to it, becoming a careening ship of Passion, pushed to and fro by their internal, non-rational variable wind and current, inevitably experiencing a series of shipwrecks. By letting it flow without guidance or direction, they become like a sailboat with the wind for a pilot, blown to and fro unto their own demise.

Teenagers are often noted for their elevated degree of passion (and recessed degree of mental "rigidity"), and it's most often spoken of as a negative thing. Aristotle speaks of it needing to be "reined in." He doesn't say it ought to be squelched or suppressed, but channeled, in the same way a wild stallion's great power is harnessed and channeled towards productivity. Although I'm no equestrian expert, I imagine a horse's wild passion can be harnessed either through breaking or wooing, the former leading to submission and mediocrity, the latter leading to mutual respect and maximum productivity. I believe the same is true of people.

The Heart produces emotions, not the least of which is desire. That's what it is designed to do. By telling it, "No," you deny your Heart's identity. You can't tell a spring not to outflow water or a songbird not to outflow song anymore than you can tell your Heart not to outflow feelings. This action flows from its identity, and we do not have the power to alter its identity. We demand a different outcome than is possible when we attempt to stop the flow of emotions.

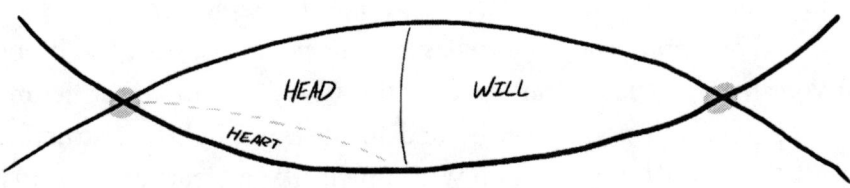

Fig. 7.5

Your Head is the seat of rationality and logic, and therefore is very rigid and structured. This structure is supposed to act as a system of courses through which your passion can flow effectively, much like blood vessels in the body *(Fig 7.5)*. Without blood vessels, blood would freely and destructively flow within you, and your Heart's amazing strength would be counter-productive.

Having a structure through which your passion can flow is just as important as having a combustion engine through which gasoline flows. If you light gasoline on fire without an engine, it explodes, which is useless at best and very destructive at worst. Within an engine, however, it can do incredible amounts of productive work.

To bring this analogy full circle, your Will is like the ignition of the gasoline in the engine. When everything is in the right position, igniting the fuel has a very positive effect. Ignition timing is very important in a combustion engine, and it's very important in decisions as well. If you run out of Passion because you've used it all on creating the structure through which it will flow, you've created a useless framework. This is called "over-planning." If however, you ignite too quickly, you burn out very quickly and you can even damage or destroy good structure in the process. A good example of this would be an unplanned creative session that runs for 48 hours straight, which then leads into two months of trying to "find inspiration." That's a typical, undisciplined internal explosion.

The appropriate internal structure is for passion, the blood of your metaphysical Heart, to flow through your rational structure, or metaphysical blood vessels, and to push through that structure at just the right time via your Will, much like a Heart beats at just the right time. That is a structure in which every internal part is acting according to its role in ordinate relationship. But even if you achieve this balance, that doesn't necessarily predicate you'll be living according to your Original Design.

As stated earlier, as your BIOS does its job from birth, a metaphysical operating system is developed at your deepest level, covering up the Spirit. This operating system, this derived identity, or "False Self" as I call it, creates artificial definitions, filters, rules, and standards that may or may not have any relevance to actual Truth.

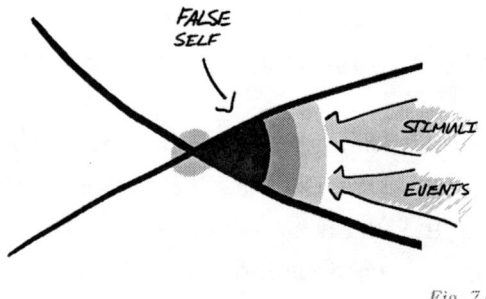

Fig. 7.6

The process by which your operating system is developed is certainly within the realm of your control, but since most people are unaware of this process, they are victims to it rather than pilots of it. The manner in which False Self is developed is much like film getting imprinted upon. You experience the outside world, and that "light" passes through your Soul, being affected by any existing beliefs, worldviews, and/or filters on the way in, and then it hits the "film" of your False Self, making an imprint on it in the shape of the event as filtered by your Soul *(Fig 7.6)*.

Naturally, the younger you are, the fewer filters you have in place, so your film is more receptive to imprinting what the outside world gives it without inhibition than it is later in life. As you age, your False Self develops in layers, building software on top of software, complexity on top of more complexity, and it quickly becomes very difficult to cut through those layers and identify root sources of behaviors.

The backdrop for your False Self "film" is your Spirit, connecting you to the spiritual realm, which means that not only can you receive imprints from the physical realm, but the spiritual realm can also influence how physical experiences imprint your False Self. I quickly come to the end of my understanding on exactly how this works, but I am confident at least, that the spiritual realm can affect how physical experiences are imprinted upon False Self.

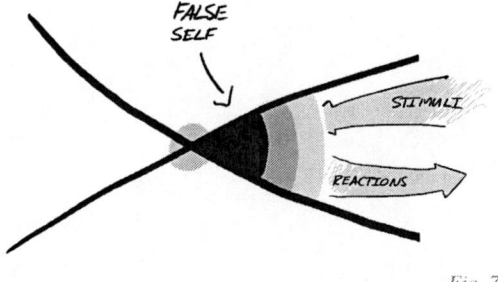

Fig. 7.7

What is most important to understand is that what has been imprinted on your False Self also acts as a root system by which filters, rules, and standards are created in your Heart and Head. And as it develops, this root system subconsciously outputs reactions to future experiences based on what has been impressed upon it in the past *(Fig. 7.7)*.

It is equally important to note that even if you connect with your Source spiritually, your False Self will not simply fall away. On the contrary, it will remain in place, and its rooted, entrenched position will block communication between you and your Origin. It will fight with all of its might to maintain dominance in your life. From that point forward, life is a painful but life-giving process of uprooting your False Self and letting your Origin flow through you, bringing you into alignment with your Original Design and your True Identity.

CHAPTER EIGHT

THE HEART

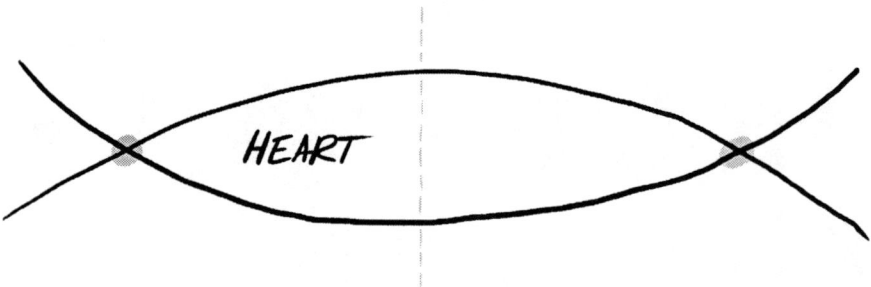

Fig. 8.1

Let's take a deeper look at the Heart, as that is frequently one of the most misunderstood components of the metaphysical Self. An essential understanding is that all Passion has an object (what you desire) and a magnitude (how much you desire it). There is a specific magnitude and object that aligns with Original Truth related to different externalities, and both or either can be out of alignment with Original Truth. For the sake of ease, I will call that which is in alignment "ordinate" and that which is not "inordinate."

We can experience a desire for an inordinate object and instead of trying to snuff it out, we can redirect towards an ordinate object. Normally, when we feel an "evil" desire, like attraction for another's spouse, we feel guilt and seek to snuff out the desire instead of redirecting that flow of Desire in the appropriate direction. When we seek to snuff it out, we hit the emergency shutoff to our Heart, cutting off our connection to Desire in order to defend against the "evil" desires.

I remember talking to a gentleman about this very issue and encouraging him to let go of his death-grip on life and allow his Heart to flow, and his response was very poignant. He said, "Kurt, you don't understand. If I let my Heart go, I would do all sorts of bad stuff." He feared his own Heart. He didn't understand what it meant to redirect and channel his Desire from inordinate things to ordinate things, and he wasn't willing to make mistakes along the way as he learned to channel his Passion effectively.

Fig. 8.2

The tough truth is that when we hit the emergency shutoff valve, we merely mute our Heart, and over time, it atrophies and reduces in strength. It keeps on transmitting and flowing Passion because that's its Identity; we just can't hear it anymore. We've really just disconnected our consciousness from it *(Fig 8.2)*. As the Heart continues to flow in this disconnected state, it floods and stagnates, often alternating between the two, destroying and breeding disease. We feel the effects of this internal fiasco, but we have no idea where it's coming from because we've become numb to its source, and we often identify (and blame) externalities as the source (e.g. our

Fig. 8.3

spouses, children, managers, clients, and other relations).

On the other end of the spectrum is the very real option to let the Heart reign instead of muting it *(Fig 8.3)*. These are people that we describe as being "controlled by their emotions." And it's true. An unrestrained Heart functions in uncontrolled "burns," like gasoline burning in the open air. It's a roller coast ride, as the unrestrained Heart experiences burnout and destructive explosions, sometimes as a cycle but often occurring simultaneously.

There are other instances of a Heart-controlled person that are less obvious. Sometimes, an individual will allow their Heart to create a rational structure around it. These are the frustrating people that are still reacting emotionally, but have a well-defined rational explanation for their emotional reaction, which obfuscates the source for both you and them. This is one of the greater challenges to unwind and bring into ordinate alignment.

Thankfully, there is a middle-ground between broken and wild Desire: Trained Desire. Damming a raging river leads to flooding, stagnation, and crippling disease; releasing it without restraint leads to unpredictable, explosive destruction; channeling it and training it leads to relentless love and fierce productivity. Depending on which extreme you're trying to curb, the approach will be different.

It's much easier to scale back from unrestraint than to recover from disengagement. The road is long and hard that faces the mess of the wreckage that has been caused by our blindness. At least we experience the wreckage in real time when we choose unrestraint. Not only do we have to face years of damage to recover from disengagement but we also have to face the fear of living differently and the pain of flexing a muscle that has long been limp.

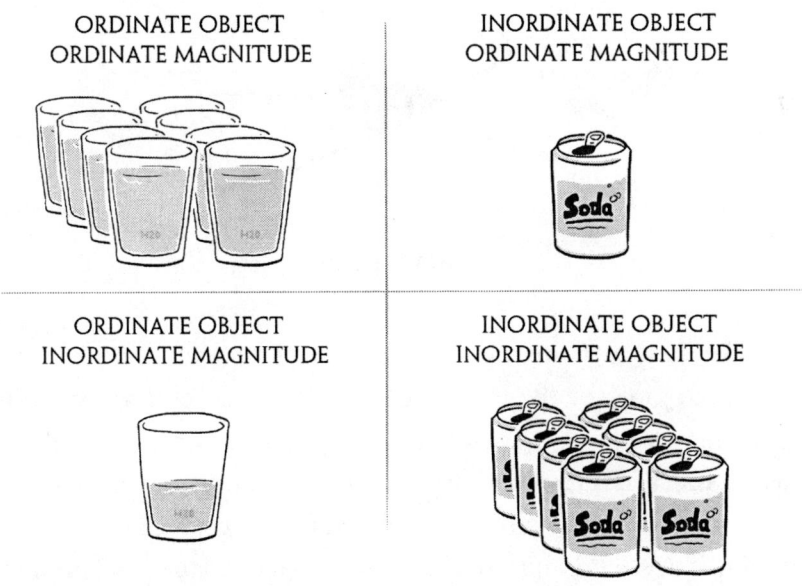

Fig. 8.4

Oftentimes, when considering whether our passion is ordinate, we merely consider the object, and as long as that is ordinate, we don't scrutinize further. Food, for example, is an entirely ordinate object of desire. We need it to live, so we have a natural and ordinate desire for it. But it is definitely possible to desire it too much or too little, which is when it becomes inordinate *(Fig 8.4)*. In the same way, sexual desire for a spouse can be inordinate if the spouse becomes a mere means to the end of gratifying the desire or if you do not desire your spouse very much. This is actually an inordinate object, though, as the gratification becomes the object rather than the spouse. While it may seem strange applied to a spouse, this is inordinate desire, and it commonly results in the spouse feeling used and inadequate.

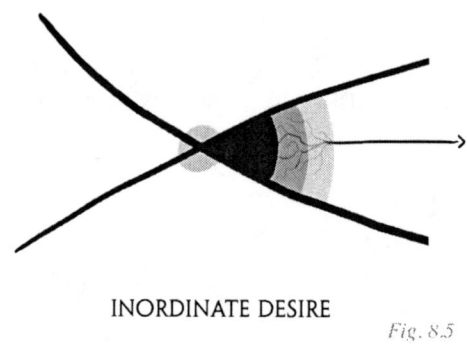

INORDINATE DESIRE

Fig. 8.5

The key to bringing inordinate Desire back into ordinate contexts is to look for the its root cause. If it's excessive Desire for food, identify why your Desire for food is so strong. Is it due to boredom, stress, depression? Every inordinate desire has a root *(Fig 8.4)*. The root will be a word of falsehood of some sort, and you have to find that falsehood and provide the truth to replace it. The falsehood could be, "I'll either be stressed and thin or happy and heavy" or, "I'm only as valuable as I am physically desirable" or, "I'm only as valuable as I am acceptable to others." There is no limit to the degree and direction of falsehood within you. And the more you understand the Truth about your Self and your proper place in relation to your environment (your family, or work, the world, the universe, etc.), the better you will be able to identify falsehood in your Self.

The process of identifying falsehood and replacing it with Truth is not remotely easy or simple. Even if you've identified the deepest root cause, the root may have had a long time to grow strong within you, so it likewise may take a fierce fight to uproot it and replace it, and possibly quite a bit of time. The falsehood won't just roll over and give up its place in you. It will fight and resist, just as a weed will resist your attempts to remove it by its roots. It may try to fool you or placate you by giving up its stem instead, but it will fight violently to defend its root. Many times you may think you've identified the root when you've only identified a more deeply seated symptom, like the stem or the leaves of a weed, and once you remove that element, you think the problem is gone, and temporarily, the symptoms vanish. But in time, it will resurface and once again choke out the good, fruit-bearing vegetation in your garden.

In fighting falsehood with Truth, what you are doing is channeling your inordinate desires to redirect away from inordinate objects and to moderate excessive or recessive intensity. It is important to note that while you cannot control the Heart's production of desire, you can control your Head. What you choose to meditate on feeds or starves the direction of desires. If you desire something inordinate, but you choose not to think upon it but instead think upon an ordinate object of that desire, you are fighting a good fight and directing your Passion down ordinate channels with ordinate intensity. The difficulty is that it actually feels "wrong" to do this, like you are withholding something good from yourself, when in reality, you are either protecting yourself from being dominated by your variable and non-rational Hearts or protecting yourself from cutting off your connection with your Heart completely.

As you direct the flows of your Hearts in ordinate directions and intensities, the flows of Desire form "channels" that grow deeper and more ingrained in you. These patterns you cultivate become much easier to maintain over time and repetition, just as a river of water flows more quickly over time as it removes obstacles and smooths out the stones in the riverbed. It's like retraining a delinquent animal, rechanneling their energy repetitively from undesirable behavior to desirable behavior. Just watch Cesar Millan at work with dogs. It's truly amazing.

So the good news is that it becomes easier over time; the bad news is that these conditioned channels apply to inordinate Desire as well. Both become more difficult to stray from and easier to remain in with time and repetition.

By understanding and adhering to these principles of the Heart, you will gain access to a reservoir of immense power within you, a power that, combined with freedom and ability, can produce extraordinary results.

My Relationship with My Heart

I started thinking about my Heart as a person inside of me with whom I have a relationship. Just recently, I realized that I have been treating my Heart very poorly. I haven't been listening to it; I have been judging it as silly, stupid, ridiculous, unreasonable, and weak; I have been ashamed of it; I have been hiding it and constantly telling it I don't need it. Imagine if that was a real person. How would a person feel if you treated it that way? The relationship would certainly not be in good shape.

About the same time I began thinking of my Heart as a person, I also realized that, consistently, we relate to other people the way we relate to our Selves, so if I want to change how I relate to others, I need to first change how I relate to my Self. Furthermore, I realized that how I relate to my own Heart is how I relate to others'

Hearts. I was blown away when I came to this conclusion. No wonder I've had challenges in my relationships!

Upon this realization, I began to connect with my Heart like I've never connected before. I stopped calling it stupid and started listening to it, started letting it flow. I danced with all my Heart for the first time in a long time, and it felt great! I had been rejecting an amazing part of me, and the truth is, I had been rejecting that part in everyone else, too. Wow. It's just as impactful to me now as it was when I first understood that. I am still steadily working on breaking a habit I formed over many years of judging people immediately on sight. Once I started noticing it, I was taken aback at how often I call people "stupid" or "loser" or "burnout" in my head. These are the words I call myself subconsciously all the time, which is why I hold others accountable to the same unforgiving standard.

Awareness is critical for me to make progress in this area. I have started building a habit of listening to my internal dialogue as I interact with and observe other people, and although it is heartbreaking to hear what I say, I have to face it and rectify those unfair judgments. By doing this consistently, I am retraining my Heart to love and accept others according to my Original Design.

CHAPTER NINE

THE HEAD

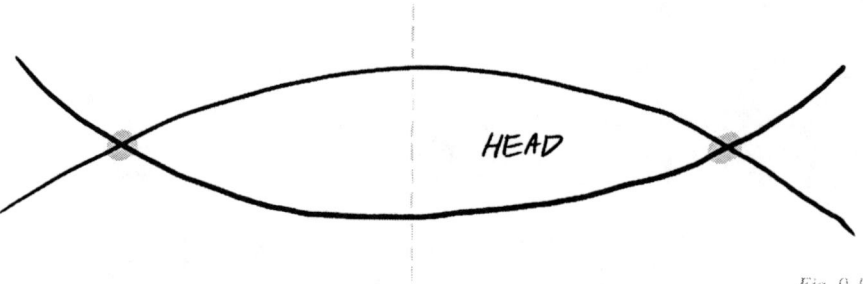

Fig. 9.1

    The Head is an incredibly powerful tool. As the seat of rational, logical thought, of data collection, analysis, and organization, and of discipline, it offers you the ability to create intentional channels for your unwavering flow of Desire and to organize your appetites appropriately, to frame your desires in such a way as to be highly productive. It is vitally important to maintaining internal balance because it is designed to be the controlling member of the human construct.

    Be aware, though, just as the Heart can become over-sized, so can the Head *(see Fig 9.2)*. An oversized Head manifests itself in observable symptoms like cynicism, which is the prioritization of science (aka the study of and dependence on the empirical or physically observable), and the inordinate denial and rejection of the immaterial (Desire, sentiment, all things spiritual, appetite, the Soul, etc.).

Fig. 9.2

In an attempt to reduce the negative effects of a wild Heart, oversized Heads will seek to squelch it completely. As we've already discussed, this is an act of futility. People with oversized Heads, including myself, have a very difficult time accepting and connecting to the immaterial realm. We're the kinds of people that deny the spiritual realm even exists because we cannot measure it, and we are uncomfortable with emotional exhibition, often considering it weakness. These are simply our own flaws that we must deal with, but should you present that to us, we would likely discount you with a pithy logical comment at best or at worst seek to tear you to pieces with a dissertation on the irrational nature of the Heart or the Spirit, applying rational arguments to non-rational components within us, which, ironically, is very irrational. But don't bring an oversized Head to the end of their logic unless you want to deal with a bit of a monster. Oversized Heads are given to rage when faced with the reality that all the time they've invested in growing their Heads, will not bring them Happiness independently, and actually now opposes their Happiness because it is inordinately bloated and imbalanced with the rest of Self.

Oversized Heads become Self-cannibals, seeking to devour any evidence that they are anything but cerebral and physical, the most tangible components of the human construct, and thus cannibalizing their immaterial Selves. Not smart, ironically.

If you identify that you are a member of this unhappy club, there is hope for you. I know because I'm in the middle of my therapeutic journey out of this inadequate salvation. It requires the diminution of focus on your Head and the growth of your immaterial parts back to ordinate, balanced sizes, as well as dealing with the inevitable mess your Heart has become with the untended flooding and stagnation that has occurred. It's a real mess, and it doesn't get cleaned up in a day. Take action: Read some good poetry, and instead of asking what the author was thinking in writing it, try to identify how the author was feeling when they wrote it. Identify the last time you felt that way. You'll probably hate this exercise at first, but it'll be good for you. Just so you know, as I write this, I'm laughing at the thought of you doing it.

The Head can also be underdeveloped or become atrophied from lack of feeding *(see Fig 8.3)*. This often happens when a person focuses inordinately on feeding their Heart and/or Body, thus leaving their Head out to dry. "Dumb blondes" and "meat heads" have both earned their names because of a group of people who have become so consumed with vanity, which is a form of approval addiction, that their Heads atrophy, and they are literally intellectually duller for it because their Heads are not being exercised. Beautiful body, flabby brain: Not a good mix.

Listening to My Head Intently

I discovered that I lacked awareness because I was so busy listening to my own Head. I literally was shifting focus from listening to another person to what my Head was saying, or what I was thinking. I still battle this unhealthy software in me. A person may say one or two sentences, and my mind will immediately begin forming a response, often in the form of a rebuttal. While they continue to speak onward, I can't hear a word they're saying, except maybe a few buzzwords that I can use to support my response. Oftentimes, when I respond, I'll either get a response like, "That's exactly what I just said," or a "We're you even listening?" The worst part of it is that I've gotten so good at this, I have preprogrammed responses to make the person believe I'm listening to them when I'm not. It's a really terrible habit.

    This doesn't just apply to conversations. I even do this when reading, watching a video, watching a demonstration or a speech... It becomes painfully clear when someone is giving instructions. I'll hear instructions 1, 2, 7, 9, and 12, but nothing in between. I was too busy thinking about instruction #2 and scrutinizing if it made sense or not to hear the next four, and so on. I'm sure you can imagine how much trouble this creates, especially since I also don't want to ask for clarification and expose the reality that I wasn't listening. So my conditioning is to "wing it" with the instructions I have and guess at what the in-between instructions are, or quietly ask someone what the missing links are, and I try to ask it with enough suavity that they're just happy I talked to them. Embarrassing, but true. This is my autopilot. All of those parts of me that I'm not aware of get run by my autopilot, which is kinda creepy. Where else in my life am I acting like an ape?

    As I became aware of my autopilot program of listening to my Head over others, I had to reckon with the truth that I place a higher value on what my Head says than on what the external source of information offers. This is foolish and highly destructive. I do not feel guilty or ashamed about it. I wasn't aware of what I was doing before, and now I am, and I'm reprogramming that behavior, which takes time, responsibility, and a healthy dose of humility.

CHAPTER TEN

THE BODY

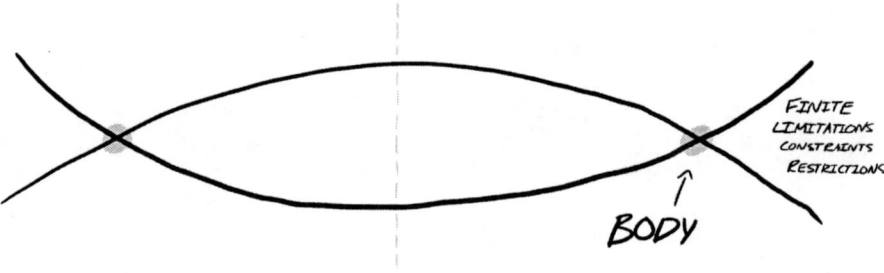

Fig. 10.1

Your Body is your point of physical interface, the seat of your physical appetites, which I collectively call "the Belly," and the seat of limitation, or the "Finite." It is through this interface that we learn about who we are and build our worldview.

Let me tell you a secret that I hope you already know: You limit yourself to an extreme degree. You let the physical world bind you to the Finite. You may even assume that the best things of life are the little pleasures you can experience through your physical interface, and so pursue those. This is the overgrowth of the Body *(Fig 10.2)*. You are born without a spiritual connection to your Origin to override and ordinately balance your physical connection, and so your Body overgrows and dominates the development of your worldview.

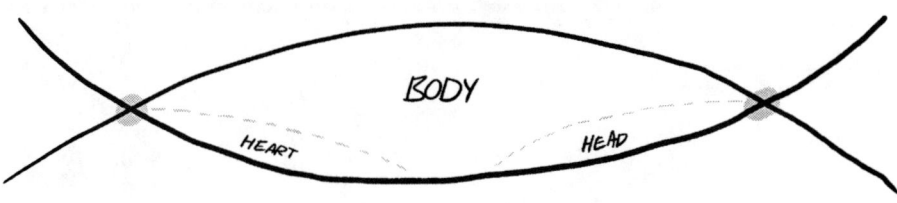

Fig. 10.2

Because your Body is the only path through which you experience the physical world, and it is the seat of your Belly and the Finite, then the Belly and the Finite often end up dominating our worldview without a counterbalance. Satisfying your Belly, your appetites for food, water, sex, comfort, and pleasure, may become your primary objective, and the Finite dictates the boundaries within which you must achieve satisfaction. Unfortunately, you will end up or have ended up feeling limited and unsatisfied in this context, understandably so, as it is a lightweight, highly limited context in which to live. Thankfully, that is not the whole of reality; in fact, it is the smallest portion of reality. Animals live fully in this context; physically-based objectives and physical limitations dominate their existence completely. Good news: You are not an animal!

Probability vs Possibility

I continue to get deeper and deeper glimpses at how much of a puppet I am. I bet I make conscious choices less than 20% of the time, and the rest of the time, I'm a product of my environment. It is my intention to invert those figures. One thing I just recently discovered is that because I am defined by a world that is finite, limited, and measured, I look at myself the same way. I view myself in

THE BODY

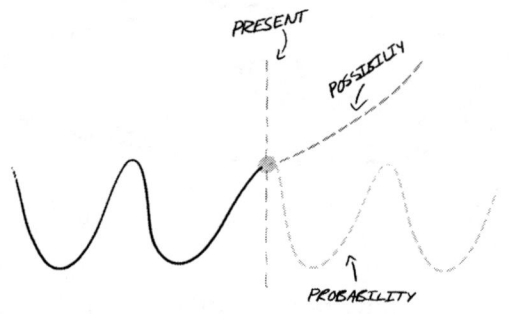

Fig. 10.3

PROBABILITY VS. POSSIBILITY

terms of my limitations, or what I can't do, based on my past experiences rather than on what is possible despite my past. As a number of my teachers have explained, it's thinking in terms of probability (the future being confined by the past) instead of possibility (the future being independent of the past and instead determined by the unlimited capacity of creativity through commitments, choices and breakthrough) *(Fig 10.3)*.

It hit me as profound that if I am defined by the physical realm, I will view myself as limited and confined, but if I am defined by my Origin, which I believe is infinite, then I will view myself as limitless; I will define myself by what is possible through growth. That was and is very inspiring to me. In the face of adversity, I used to say, "Poor me. Guess I can't go there." Now, when adversity rears its head, I have the opportunity to say, "Bring it on! I can conquer and overcome even this!" Is that how I always respond now? Wellllll… no. I must admit I still default to the easier limiting response, or I'll use one of my favorite escapes, "They couldn't possibly expect me to achieve this now! They'll understand." See? "They." When I say this, I'm still looking for my justification, my validation, from the outside world. "They" is an imaginary group of people in my head that I'm perpetually trying to impress. There's probably a diagnosis for this.

CHAPTER ELEVEN

THREE KEYS TO PRODUCTIVITY

PASSION, FREEDOM, ABILITY

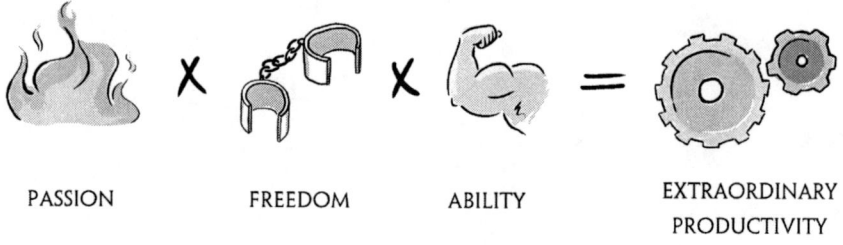

PASSION FREEDOM ABILITY EXTRAORDINARY PRODUCTIVITY

Fig. 11.1

There are three fundamental components to being extraordinarily productive: Passion, Freedom, and Ability, the first of which we've already discussed at length *(Fig 11.1)*.

Freedom

Freedom is one of the most misunderstood concepts in our culture. The pervasive understanding of the term is "able to do whatever one wants." While this is true in a sense, the way it is understood is deeply flawed. I will restructure the definition to bring out the essential meaning: "Authority over one's self; autonomy; Self-sovereign."

As Maslow accurately points out in his "Hierarchy of

Needs," we humans need more than just food, water, and shelter. We are not merely organic Bodies. We have needs of the Soul and Spirit. We need to know our Origin, Identity, and Purpose; we need to experience intimate relationship with others; we need to fulfill our purpose and live from our true Identity. We need to be who we really are.

Many people seem to maintain the assumption that it is ordinate to get that stuff "after work." They get the material resources they need at work, which allows them to experience the "other stuff" when they're not at work. Essentially, they assume that people can accept that nearly half their lives are spent supporting the lowest forms of existence, that half their day is spent being thought of as merely commodity, merely material, just as lumber is material. Do you think of yourself as a human resource?

Do you think of yourself as a human resource? Do you think of others as resources? Objects? Obstacles?

My goal is to invite the entire individual into the work environment, Body, Soul, and Spirit. That's a major step towards cultivating freedom, and it doesn't inhibit productivity at all. People appreciate having permission to be fully themselves at work. It's horrible to feel empty or fake while at work. I think managers are ill-equipped and afraid to deal with the immaterial aspects of their team members, and moreover, they think it is wasted time and effort because these intangibles aren't obviously connected with the tangible goods and services they offer. The tendency is always to fear and reject what we do not understand, and that is the primary driving force behind this leave-yourself-at-the-door policy.

The problem with this policy is that freedom and responsibility are directly proportionate: When one rises, the other does as well and vice versa. So when you repossess a team's freedom to be fully themselves, you repossess their responsibility as well. Or from a different angle, you can't hand a child all of their freedom at once, nor can you hand an immature adult all of their freedom at once. Because with that full freedom comes full responsibility, and a child or immature adult would be crushed by full responsibility. Most adults have not been trained through childhood to support and sustain a full, adult level of responsibility.

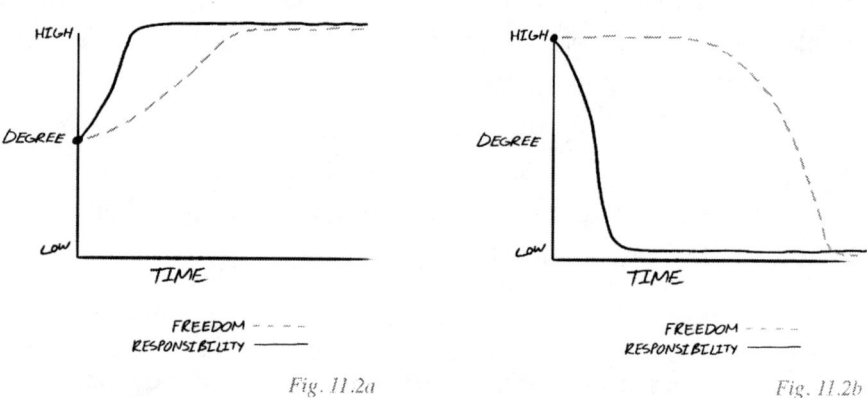

Fig. 11.2a   *Fig. 11.2b*

You can see this on a national level as well as an individual level. As people lose their ability or their desire to take responsibility, they start to lose their freedom. Freedom's response lags behind an individual's or generation's choice and ability to take responsibility, as one generation's embrace of responsibility "purchases" a certain degree of freedom for one or more descending generations. You can see this even more practically in the reality that, often, your choices to take responsibility are not immediately met with an increase in freedom, but take time to "purchase" freedom *(see Fig 11.2a)*. Likewise, if you have a certain freedom, but choose not to or are not able to be responsible for it, you will experience the benefits of this freedom for a short period of time while your lack of responsibility for it will cause it to diminish and eventually disappear *(see Fig 11.2b)*. Material wealth, the freedom of money, is one of the easiest practical manifestations of this truth. If you don't have wealth, taking on more responsibility in ways that positively affect your wealth will produce it, but only if you maintain that responsibility for a sufficient length of time. Conversely, if you already possess great money freedom, but do not take responsibility for the maintenance of it, you can still experience the benefits of it for a while before it disappears. See the figures above for a visual explanation.

Also, the more responsibility you ably assume in alignment with a particular freedom, the faster you will acquire it. It is the difference between the "maintenance" level of responsibility and the assumed level of responsibility divided by the magnitude of external resistance that determines how quickly you breakthrough static friction and your rate of acceleration towards freedom.

(Assumed Responsibility − "Maintenance" Level Responsibility) / External Resistance Factor = Rate of Acceleration Toward Greater Freedom *(see figure below)*

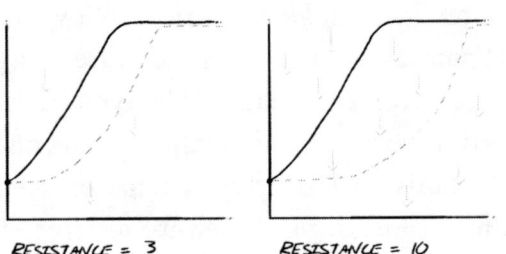

RESISTANCE = 3   RESISTANCE = 10   *Fig. 11.3*

For instance, a poor person who was willing and able to take on a great deal more responsibility in alignment with increasing the freedom of material wealth would move toward that freedom much faster in the United States than in Sudan because the external resistance to the poor acquiring material freedom is far greater in Sudan than in the United States *(Fig 11.3)*.

Everyone has access to freedom; few are aware of the cost. When a mother and father toil and sweat much of their lives to elevate their family and obtain freedom from poverty, they may fail to teach their children what it takes to maintain such freedom, and their children will embrace the freedom without embracing the responsibility that comes with it. The injustice of the whole deal is that the children may experience freedom from poverty all of their lives and then pass the bondage of poverty back to their children. So also it can be said that bondage lags behind an individual's or generation's decadence, as one generation's decadence purchases a certain degree of bondage for descending generations.

But bondage is a good teacher. It teaches you how much more you need than what you have been able to access, and that should keep you humble. In fact, if freedom has been purchased for you by past generations, the moment you become proud and selfish in your freedom, you begin to trek down the path of decadence, the path that returns to bondage. It is an inescapable human cycle of the painful, hard purchase of freedom and the decadent squandering of freedom by ignorant, selfish beneficiaries, followed by a period of sobriety and the painful, hard re-purchase of freedom.

The phrase, "You don't know what you have until you lose it," is particularly relevant to this matter. It seems as if humans naturally tend towards the opposite extreme on the pendulum arc between freedom and bondage. When we are free, we don't know or forget what we have, so we don't value it and take the necessary responsibility to protect and maintain it; then, when we lose our freedom and are bound, we are willing to go through far more pain to regain it because the painful experience of bondage provides a very cogent repulsion that acts as the energy in the opposite direction, just like a pendulum swing or a stretched rubber band. We swing between the extremes of: 1. Despising our position and fighting against it until we've obtained the opposite and 2. Becoming lax once we've obtained it and letting it slip through our fingers. We are truly short-sighted creatures.

The only alternative path is the path of contentment, to be in a position of peace, balance, and rest despite your circumstances, or to experience constant internal freedom despite external influences. Much good writing exists on this matter already, so I will not diverge into it.

Freedom and bondage have internal and external sources. Internal freedom and bondage, such as knowledge, ignorance, wisdom, and folly, cannot be affected for good or ill in any way by an external source without the consent of the possessor. It can be offered and cultivated externally, but it must be received internally by the possessor; as they say, "You can lead a horse to water, but you can't make it drink."

External freedom and bondage, including resources, travel, physical privacy, and geographic habitation, can be affected for good or ill by external sources without the consent of the affected party. If someone else steals from you, it affects your freedom of resources without your consent. Passports affect your freedom of travel without your personal consent. Property taxes affect your freedom of geographic habitation with or without your individual consent. There are so many external, non-consensual forces affecting your external freedom, it is ignorant to believe you are in control of your external environment.

Internal and external freedom requires an act of giving permission. Internal freedom requires you to give permission to yourself. External freedom requires that one or many others give you permission. Freedom and permission are essentially interchangeable. I bring it up now because there are lingual nuances present in the word "permission" that I think are important to capture in understanding what it means to be free.

For instance, surrender is the act of giving yourself permission to let go of some control in one sense and to gain even greater control in a deeper sense. Oftentimes, people do not give themselves permission to do certain things because they've experienced hurt through those activities before; by denying themselves, they prevent pain, and thus are in control of that particular source of pain. Take, for example, a romantic relationship that fails and leaves both members deeply hurt. Both will undoubtedly be fearful about experiencing such pain again and therefore will have a natural resistance to engaging in a romantic relationship again. If they choose not to, they feel in control of the situation. They've made a decision that will prevent their being hurt in the same way again. But in reality, they are not in control; they have subjected themselves to their fear and are being controlled by it (more on this in Chapter 24). Typically, you are most in control when you do things least natural to you. It is then that you really experience the full depth of your sovereignty over your Self. When hurt, the natural response is to recoil, but what if you gave yourself permission to remain in that state and acted against your natural impulse? Wouldn't you be in greater control of yourself at that point?

Obviously, you can apply this principle inappropriately.

There are appropriate times to yield to instinct, but there is a difference between autopilot yielding and proactive yielding. I'm merely recommending the latter.

Ability

While Ability is essential for productivity, it results from Passion and Freedom working together effectively. With Passion flowing through a quality, disciplined structure, you will undoubtedly wax in your abilities at an accelerated rate. It is a powerful byproduct of establishing a well-ordered internal structure. I will not belabor it further. It's that simple.

CHAPTER TWELVE

THE BELLY AND APPETITE

When I think about freedom, I can't help but think of the movie Braveheart, in which Mel Gibson portrays the Scottish peasant William Wallace who leads a revolution against Longshanks, the king of England. The two most moving moments in the movie revolve around the desire for freedom. Wallace is intensely focused on his pursuit of freedom, and he is willing to give all of himself for it. While at first, his rebellion is for revenge, his Heart changes, and his motive becomes a belief in the human choice for freedom and the importance of making that choice at all costs. He is willing to die for freedom, and he proves it many times throughout the story.

For years before Wallace led the rebellion against England, the people of Scotland desired freedom from the heavy hand of Longshanks, but most were not willing to pursue it at all costs. They were not united in freedom. Only when Wallace took the first step and put his stake solidly in the gorund did his countrymen stand behind him and fight.

I see so much of that reality in today's world. Most modern-day "leaders," whether knowingly or ignorantly, are like the Scottish nobles who compromise with Longshanks and use their power to gain more for themselves. They think that fighting against a power so great as Longshanks would be futile and counterproductive. So they take the bones he tosses them and feed their armies well to keep them content.

It's the same with leadership today. Instead of embracing ideals, we view the ideal as unfeasible and absurd. The people you lead couldn't handle being free, you think. They would just lie around and do nothing all the time, or they would focus only on the tangential stuff that they wanted to do and cease to be materially productive. If you're the only person you lead, you very well might withhold freedom from yourself because you fear you couldn't handle it. These concerns are entirely reasonable, and it's completely possible, even likely, that those you lead would become completely unproductive if given freedom without structure. Those who respond unproductively to freedom should be evaluated on a case-by-case basis to determine whether to attempt to invite them into productive freedom or to replace them.

Unfortunately, most managers turn to fear and food to motivate those they lead, hovering silent threats over their heads in case they aren't productive and giving them material incentives to be productive. But they haven't captured the Hearts of those whom they lead. Not even close. Can you imagine the Scottish peasant armies becoming an unstoppable force because the nobles offer them an extra ration of food if they work hard or threaten them with a whipping if they don't? This approach will not produce extraordinary results, nor will it last very long in producing even a semblance of the desired affect.

We know it is possible for human beings to be self-motivated, to have something from within them propel them forward, and yet we continue to act as if it is impossible, giving our armies fear and food for their service.

Appetite

Understanding human appetite is fully relevant to leading Self because we so commonly seek to motivate ourselves through the satisfaction of appetites. So I think it is fitting to clarify and discuss the form and operation of appetite, how our present leadership culture uses appetite to motivate people, the outcome of that mode of motivation, and an alternative to it.

An appetite is any desire that, once satisfied, is desired again. There are physical appetites like sleep, nutrition, and sex; there are Heart-based appetites like achievement and approval; there can even be Head-based appetites like creativity and critical engagement. Appetite is like a slowly (or not-so-slowly) draining sink that you must refill constantly. You fill it up, and it drains back out and must be refilled again and again perpetually. This is the cycle of appetite. Motivation through appetite satisfaction is a cycle that never ends, and it's also a cycle that is always diminishing in effectiveness. What once was extremely satisfying now merely maintains.

Aristotle points out that pain is present in the absence of appetite satisfaction, and the greatest pleasure is found not in being satisfied, but in the process of becoming satisfied. It is painful when we cannot satisfy our appetite, and it is pleasurable to satisfy each of them.

Another important aspect of appetite that is essential to understand is that the frequency and magnitude of satisfaction of an appetite makes that appetite grow or diminish relative to what it is accustomed to. In other words, if you're used to eating meager portions twice a day and then you shift to eating three sumptuous portions daily, initially, the shift will be received as abundance, but as this diet is maintained, your appetite for food will grow and you will require more food to satisfy it, so if you went back to eating meager portions twice a day, what once satisfied you would no longer.

Although Relativists reading this will have a problem with me saying so, there is an ordinate level of satisfaction for each appetite, and excessive or deficient satisfaction of each appetite is called deviance because you're deviating from the ordinate satisfaction of appetite. The ordinate level may change according to circumstances, but there is always an ordinate level of satisfaction for each set of variables. For instance, if all you have is one piece of bread for a family meal, your ordinate portion will differ from what would be ordinate if you had a table full of food. Eating a full piece of bread in the former circumstance would be excessive while it would be deficient in the latter.

Finally, there are varying levels of pleasure and pain according to the contrast between the means by which appetite is typically satisfied by an individual and the means by which they currently satisfy it. The degree of pleasure experienced from higher forms of satisfaction diminishes the more you experience it, and that is relative to what the individual is accustomed to. If a person is used to eating bugs to satisfy their hunger, and they then have the opportunity to satisfy their hunger through a quality, home-cooked meal, they will experience a very high level of pleasure from this satisfaction because it so starkly contrasts with their standard of satisfaction in a positive way. However, an aristocrat accustomed to eating the finest of cuisine cooked by the best chefs in the world would likely find a quality, home-cooked meal merely adequate at best, and furthermore, they would find bugs as simply unpalatable for the satisfaction of their hunger because it contrasts so extremely with their standard of satisfaction.

If the bug-eater switches places with the aristocrat, he will eventually become accustomed to the gourmet cuisine and the intensity of pleasure will recede with each meal. The aristocrat, having switched places, will refuse to eat for a great length of time until the extremity of the appetite's lacking overcomes the contrast between bugs and his customary food. While this inevitability of accepting substandard satisfaction is true of many of the appetites, it is most true of those that are unavoidable or necessary for life, such as sleep and food.

The current standard of leadership promotes using the satisfaction of appetite to motivate people to serve. It is an exchange, a transaction, giving people the means by which they can satisfy their appetites (usually money) in exchange for their service. To convey the nonsensical nature of this method, consider a man whose sole goal is to satisfy every appetite on demand outside of the eight hours he works. He wants to fulfill his appetite for any kind and quantity of food, comfort, sex, and other appetites. He is committed to realizing all of his wildest dreams and fantasies. Provided the man has no personal restraint outside of protecting his life and other instincts, what happens to him? He becomes addicted to these pleasures, and he bloats his capacity and demand for them. It's just like many addictive drugs in that you always need a little bit more for the same trip. Would he ever be complete? No. The sink always drains and requires more. What appeared at first to be his salvation would end up being bondage. Before too long, every waking moment would be controlled by his appetites, and he would become a slave to them. He would seek to fill his ever-growing needs and all of his life would be spent seeking the extra he needs to overcome the ever-increasing threshold of mere maintenance.

Obviously, this is not the kind of person you want to be, nor is the kind of person you want to engage with in a productive capacity. You will never be able to give them enough resources to fulfill all of their appetites because, by nature, the appetites are insatiable. The moment one is fulfilled, it begins to recede back towards unfulfillment. And the trouble is, there are so many to fulfill, you would end up scurrying back and forth between them all trying to survive. Having insatiable needs is dangerous; if you have such needs and do not change course, eventually, you will get desperate, and desperate people are dangerous.

Eventually, addicts stop thinking about tripping on whatever it is they're addicted to and become fixated on mere survival, mere maintenance of their appetites. And beyond that, they fail to even manage maintenance and experience breakdown, for better or worse. When I say "addicts," I'm not just referring to drug addicts; I'm also referring to addicts of alcohol, sex, pseudo-intimate relationships, knowledge, approval, video games, food, sports, work, television, achievement, or anything else that can give a short-lived sense of satisfaction and needs to be refilled.

Notice I haven't mentioned money as an addiction. It cannot be an addiction because it is meaningless in and of itself. For most, money means getting the products and services they want and need. And for some, it also is an indicator of achievement, a measuring stick. These are the people that many view as addicted to money, when they're actually addicted to achievement. They've just become so fixated on money as their prime measurement of achievement that it appears they are addicted to money. In truth, I may have named other secondary addictions above which are really a means to deeper addictions, so that is something you can review and consider (e.g. Is knowledge a prime addiction or the means to approval?)

However, money is oftentimes the connecting point between us and the fulfillment of our appetites, so when anyone speaks of wanting or needing money, understand they are really referring to what money indicates or acquires for them as the real need or want. Our desire for money can behave similarly to our desire for the objects of our appetites because it is so closely tied to the acquisition of those objects. The only way we can be satisfied with how much money we have is if we gain control of our appetites and derive satisfaction from an alternative source. Your appetite will never be satisfied completely and therefore will never be the means to your full satisfaction.

On the upside, your appetites can be the source of a great deal of ordinate sweetness in life. In and of themselves, they are not bad or wrong in any way. But they so often become a source of bondage when you feed them or starve them inordinately.

While it seems counterintuitive, true Freedom exists only in the presence of your Head establishing and reinforcing strong boundaries and structure that confine and restrain. Within these boundaries, you are completely free. Without them, you fall into bondage. But as you grow in strength, your boundaries will broaden and you will experience freedom proportionate to your ability and will to be a responsible steward of it. This is the ordinate structure within which to expand your freedom. You can't handle boundless freedom because it requires infinite responsibility.

"Hi. My Name Is Kurt. And I'm an Addict."

I'm a perpetually recovering addict. I am addicted to many things in my life, but most insidiously pervasive has been my addictions to approval and to being right. And just like the worst of them, at the peak of my addiction, I would have told you there was nothing out of place. I was fine. I had all sorts of ways to explain it so that it sounded to me like I was a reasonable, balanced person. And most people bought my story. But I was addicted. Everything I did was either touched by it or directly controlled by it.

I love approval and attention. And there's nothing wrong with that. Approval and attention are awesome. But my appetite for these twins was over-fed, and it bloated and expanded into an addiction over time. Once it became an addiction, I subconsciously built a "character" that would get more approval and attention. I performed well in this role I created, at least for a while. It seemed to be working for me. I was getting the thumbs up, and life was good.

But eventually, the energy it took to maintain this performance was overwhelming, and it began to break down. Even then, I deftly reacted, and embraced failure as a part of my persona, emphasizing the value of failure and how much I was learning from it. I would bounce back after each failure, blazing forward like a true entrepreneur. Nothing could keep me from looking good. Or so I thought.

Eventually, after eight business failures in four years, I hit a wall. I was just faking it, and I couldn't avoid it anymore. Unfortunately, at the time, I believed I was living authentically, and I didn't realize it was my inauthentic misrepresentation that was producing such poor results. So, while it did shatter my contrived image of the rockstar entrepreneur, it also planted a seed of doubt in me that I wasn't capable of success. If you had asked me at the time, I wouldn't have said I was defeated, but my actions told another tale.

Even though I had assumed some bad perspective with the good, it did redirect me enough to begin to produce vocational success in my life. I stopped trying to be the got-it-all-figured-out rockstar, and instead focused on helping others be successful to the best of my abilities. That was an important turning point for me. I hadn't kicked my addiction. I had just broken through one of its many layers.

My addiction to being right created very similar results and went hand-in-hand with my addiction to approval. I believed that if I could be right all of the time, then everyone would approve of me. And I believed it with such conviction that I tried to be right all the time for years and years, and produced a sizable graveyard of failed initiatives along the way.

This addiction has stayed with me very strongly, and I am now actively working on breaking through it and retraining my internal processes. I have been so committed to being right (to feed my addiction) that I don't even listen to most of what other people are saying. Instead, after they say one or two sentences, I immediately start thinking about what I think about what they're saying and how I'll respond. It's totally messed up. They could say fifteen more sentences while I sit there and ponder the first two sentences, all the while my autopilot response is, "Uh huh? Yeah. Right. Yeah. Uh huh…" I've trained myself so well that I actually make them believe that I am listening to them when I haven't the faintest idea what they're saying. It only works when I'm lucky (or unlucky, depending on how you look at it). Much of the time, I give my response, and they say, "Were you even listening to what I said? I *just* said that." I'm quite talented at squirming out of such situations and making myself look intelligent and worthy of approval.

But let's face it. I'm sick. And I mean that. I have a disease, and it's a disease that is eating my relationships and business opportunities alive. Now that I'm aware of it, I am actively addressing it, but it takes effort and focus to even be aware of it, much less make a different choice. I realized how unaware I was after some powerful challenges from people I appreciate very much. Not only do I not listen to others, but I'm absorbed in whatever I'm doing at any given time, and I can't even imagine how many opportunities have been screaming right in my face, and I've been completely oblivious. Oblivious. That's a word that describes my life for the past decade quite nicely. I have been comfortably couched in oblivion. I have benefited by having a big, fat excuse for my failures and inconsistencies. "Oh, I didn't hear you." "Sorry, I was totally unaware." "Whoops, I must have missed that one." It sounds like a genuinely honest mistake, and that's why it took so long to identify in me. It works like a charm. I fooled even me.

Since becoming aware of this addiction and corresponding autopilot program, I have made some major changes, and I'm just now starting to experience the incredible abundance I have been missing out on for so many years. I grieve what I might have gained, and I am grateful for enlightenment and graduation to a new level now.

I have to face the brutal facts, though. If these areas of my life were hidden from me, how many more will I discover in the coming years? I know there are many more levels and layers. And the more and more I realize that, the more and more committed I am to getting real with myself and inviting feedback from others who can see my programs better than I can. I strongly recommend you do the same.

One final note. As C.S. Lewis so eloquently put it, the Head rules the Belly through the Heart.* The Heart provides the horsepower by which the Head, through its healthy structure, rules our appetites and maintains their satisfaction within ordinate boundaries. Without well-conditioned sentiments backing up your Head's intentions, you cannot lead yourself.

---

* Abolition of Man, by C.S. Lewis

CHAPTER THIRTEEN

THE WILL

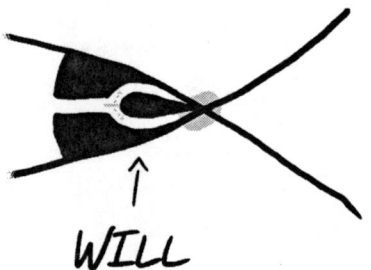

Fig. 13.1

The Will is an incredibly powerful member of your personhood. In a sense, it is the single most powerful member. It is like the tiny rudder that steers the massive ship. The ability to choose is deeply undervalued by our global society as a whole. We get to choose what we say, what we do, and what we think. Stop for a moment and consider what I just said. If you really stepped into that power and changed what you say, do, and think, your whole life would be transformed in an instant.

In one capacity, the Will operates very much like a spark plug. In short, it is your decision-making member. In its ordinate context, it ignites the fuel of Passion at a timing defined by the Head. Your Will is like a muscle that is trained by your Head. But your Will yields to whichever member is in control at the time whether that be your Heart, Body, Head or Spirit. As long as your Head is directing traffic, though, your Will aligns with and is trained by it.

Unfortunately, the Will is commonly a neglected or abused

child. Instead of embracing and leveraging its power, most resort to autopilot and rarely even use their Will, except to choose which flavor of ice cream to buy or which show to watch. We've reduced kingly power and authority to a beggar's request. We've abandoned the Will as a valuable asset within us, some for comfort, some from fear, still others from ignorance. Just making that single change and tapping into the power of the Will on a pandemic scale would generate such an outpouring of power, we wouldn't recognize our own planet.

People also abuse their Will. Frequently, people lack or cannot access Passion for something they want to accomplish, so instead of rectifying their lack of Desire, they force it with sheer Willpower. To be clear, the Will is meant to "force" action, but just enough to let your Passion gain adequate traction to propel you forward independently of the Will. In this way, the Will is very much like a starter motor. When you turn the key in your car, you are engaging the starter motor, which is an electrically-driven motor that gets things moving just long enough to start the combustion process. In the same way, the Will gets things in motion just long enough for your Passion to ignite with adequate magnitude and rhythm to maintain and grow the motion.

Combustion engines were not designed to run solely on electricity. You can actually put older manual transmission vehicles in gear with an empty gas tank and turn the key in the ignition, and the vehicle will lurch forward and "drive" running solely off the starter motor. (My dad used this trick one time when we ran out of gas 50 feet from the gas station.) This is precisely what happens when we try to employ Will as a means of propulsion when it's intended to be a means of initiation. If you do this consistently, you will either burn

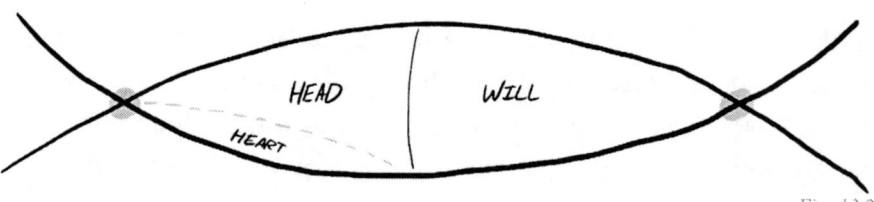

Fig. 13.2

out, and your Will will become impotent in the same way an electric motor will burn out and become useless, or your Will will become overgrown and its strength will offer you the unhappy opportunity to permanently replace your Heart's ordinate role *(Fig 13.2)*.

After initiating, if Passion doesn't readily build, you may need to figure out why your gas tank is empty or why the gas is getting blocked from the combustion chamber. You might be trying to force yourself to do something you weren't designed to do and your Heart is letting you know. Then again, you may just need to press on and complete the task before you. It's easy to use "lack of passion" as an excuse not to do difficult things that you certainly are designed to do. But if you find that you lack Passion for something over a long period of time and you are constantly "grinding" your way through it via Willpower, you may need to stop and re-evaluate the pursuit. Maybe you are forcing yourself to be an accountant when you were designed to be an artist or vice versa.

Bear in mind, however, that you can quickly get into a very toxic mindset if you start determining if you were designed to do things based on if you "feel" like it or not. If you judge by that criterion, you will come to believe you weren't designed to do anything that requires any effort… and that's called being a loser.

Please, do not use the principle that Passion is supposed to be your propellant as an excuse to not complete important tasks and keep commitments just because Passion isn't present. Ideally, you would be able to connect your Heart's power to whatever task you were working on that was in alignment with your Identity, but sometimes, for whatever reason, we get disconnected. But the task is still important in the grand scheme of things. You may need to push through on Willpower alone in the knowledge that the task is truly in alignment with who you are. The need to address a disconnection from your Heart is specifically relevant if it becomes systemic, at which point it becomes unsustainable.

Your Will serves a second function as well. Just as it does short-term pushes to initiate, it also acts as a guide to maintain a course. This is what we commonly call Focus. I'm sure you've experienced it many times when you're trying to get something done, but there are all manner of distractions calling to you, which will delay or completely supplant the completion of the more important task you are working on. There are two variables that determine whether you stay on course or not: The strength of your Passion for the task, sourced from your Heart, and the strength of your Discipline, which is another word for Willpower. If your Will is weak, your Passion will break out of your Head's structure and spill into other less productive or unproductive capacities just as a blood vessel breaks and bruises. If you have weak Passion, you're already running on Willpower, and its strength will determine if you can complete the task.

Focus is the extension of your Discipline that is manifested when you are tempted to be distracted or divert from your present course. Focus will deflect the temptation, or if you've diverted already, it will draw you back on course. Just a moment ago while I was writing this section, my Skype pinged me, letting me know I had a message. If I had weaker Discipline in that moment, my

THE WILL

curiosity would have overpowered me, and I would have taken a peek. Even in this moment, there's a degree of burning curiosity. But I have disciplined myself to stay focused, especially because I have committed to complete this book by a specific date, and I only have so much time each day to write.

Do not underestimate the power of focus. It will make all of your time more productive and therefore more valuable. Distractions seek to destroy the value of your time. They are not your friends. Do not answer when they call.

The Will is the key to extraordinary results. The ability to choose what we do, what we think, what we say… That is all the power we need to transform the world.

PART THREE
WHAT A LEADER IS

CHAPTER FOURTEEN

WHAT DOES A LEADER DO?

LEADERSHIP REVOLVES AROUND GROWING, BEING CREATIVE, AND SERVING OTHERS.

Your Original Design is to be a leader. But that Identity is likely having a difficult time making it to the outside world. It is important to be able to identify when your actions do and do not reflect your Original Design so you can find and rectify the sources of those actions that are not in alignment with who you really are. This is not only applicable to self-reflection, but it is also highly relevant to helping others see themselves. Besides that, I'm sure that by this point, you are ready for some practical clarity.

You can identify true leadership in others and yourself through a number of "observables." Likewise, you can identify lack of true leadership by the absence or opposites of these observables.

At a very top level, we are designed to be good. By "good," I mean "good" as it has been defined for ages. Being selfless, caring about others, serving others, honesty, patience, gentleness, longsuffering, joy, hope, kindness, compassion, creativity, etc. etc. etc. The great thing is that everyone already knows these things are good. How we know that and where the definition of "good" originates are great inquiries, but for the sake of keeping things more or less focused, I'll save that for a later discussion, perhaps even in a later book. For now, you will just have to be satisfied that we are correct in our understanding of "good," and that we are designed to be good. The Purpose of every leader is quite simple: To grow, to be creative, and to serve others.

Grow

Think of yourself like the branch of a grapevine, the vine being your Origin and you extending from it. If you, as the branch, yield to the vine, you will grow and bear fruit. If you do not let the vine flow through you, you will atrophy and produce no fruit. The branch of a grapevine is designed to let the vine sustain and grow it. In the same way, we are designed to let our Origin sustain and grow us through our Spirit, but unfortunately, most of us spend our time seeking sustenance and growth from the outside world, which cannot give us either.

To grow is to increase your capacity by which Spiritual Life can flow through you and produce more fruit, which, for the sake of simplicity, is the "good" we discussed above. That is the purpose of growth: To produce more fruit.

If growth results in just more foliage, it is worthless growth. But many people prefer the outward appearance of foliage to actual fruit production. A vinedresser will cut back a vine to a stub every year so as to improve its yield the following year, but you can resist the cutting, reducing knife of the vinedresser in your life so as to maintain the appearance of growth all the time. Then all of your energy is spent maintaining your foliage, and you do not have enough energy to produce any good, usable fruit. Are you spending all of your energy maintaining your appearance? If you are, it is because you are dependent on what others think of you for your sense of worth. Maybe you are addicted to approval or maybe you're hiding shame behind the foliage; either way, you are wasting your life as a result. Cut it out (clever pun intended)! People who have experienced significant growth seem to be especially vulnerable to this as people begin to notice how fruitful and strong their branch is; in a moment of self-indulgence, their focus can shift from producing fruit to producing "plumage." It is a sad waste of so much productive capacity. So, as you experience growth and find success in producing much fruit, beware lest you fall into this temptation. It's the fastest way to waste all of your hard work and diligence on supporting your false image.

One final note I think is very important to recognize. A branch of a grapevine does not eat its own fruit. It grows the fruit for others to enjoy. Don't get confused about the nature of fruit. You aren't producing it primarily for your own enjoyment, but for others. Your primary enjoyment comes from the production of it, from the joy of being who you really are and fulfilling your Purpose accordingly.

Create

The majority of people put creativity in a box (which is an oxymoron) by believing it is something certain types of people are and others are not. In reality, being creative merely means creating new things. You are creative. Even if you're a mathematician, you are still creative. You have to creatively move numbers around in order to achieve an intended result, and by moving those numbers around, you create a new outcome. That's creativity at work, just as much as painting a picture of a land that doesn't exist is creative. I believe your creativity is a reflection of our Origin's love for creating. It's imprinted upon you from birth. It is your birthright to create. Children understand this without being taught. They create worlds around them that only they can see. They tote guns that don't exist and shoot wild animals that aren't really there, all the while riding a black stallion when others merely see a park bench. You were born creative. It is the vulgarity of the adult world that crushes it and clams it up, but it's still there, hoping to generate new things in your life.

Being creative is essential to good growth. You cannot grow without stepping outside of your comfort zone, your safe area, and you cannot survive outside of your comfort zone without creativity. You must become more resourceful than you've ever been in places you've never been doing things you've never done, and that requires a great deal of creativity. If you don't think you're creative, put yourself in a position where creativity is demanded and commit to following through. If you choose not to fully commit, you'll just find more evidence that you're not creative, so don't waste your time. Complete commitment is key. Only then will you discover how creative you really are. More on this later.

Serve

As clarified in the vine analogy, we produce fruit for the benefit of others. Our purpose is to connect and yield to the Vine, our Source, and to produce fruit for others. That is our right place in this world. Many people have a hard time with this one. There is such a strong pull in us to serve ourselves, that it can easily sound like a terrible way to live. These people think they know what they want, and serving others as a fundamental goal is in opposition to what they think will make them happy. As paradoxical as it might sound, though, by sacrificing our own selfish interest in service to others, we get what we really want. It's pretty awesome.

> Our mission at Classy Llama Studios, which we embrace with the utmost seriousness, is to fearlessly, sustainably serve others with wild abandon in ever-increasing breadth and depth.

CHAPTER FIFTEEN

NATURAL ORDER

I get to share a beautiful truth with you. By doing good business, I aligned with my Original Design, and in so doing, I came into alignment with Natural Order. Natural Order is the intended system, the way things were intended to work according to Original Design. And the awesome reality is that when you act against who you really are, including living life in pursuit of your egocentric desires, what you want slips from you fingers; but when you live according to who you really are, what you want overtakes you in abundance. This is Natural Order. The more fully you step into who you really are and live from that core context, the more abundant your life will be. Or put another way, your results will make it clear whether you're living according to Original Design. The outward reflects the inward.

The reason I'm writing this book is not because I want to sell millions of copies and become disgustingly famous and wealthy, although that would be nice. I'm writing this book because I believe it contains truths that are critically important for you to understand. Practically speaking, it is certainly possible that a well-written book that reveals important truths to many people might produce prosperity and notoriety for the author. But that's not the point. If only one person read it and was transformed as a result, it would justify the 200+ hours it took to write, edit, and publish it all. But if it manages to initiate transformation in hundreds or thousands of people, then my time is massively leveraged in building abundant value into the lives of others. You see, part of my personal mission is to fearlessly, sustainably build value into the lives of others with ever-increasing breadth and depth, so I must constantly be looking for ways to better leverage my talent, skills, wisdom, and experience. "Ever-increasing breadth and depth" is a tall order, one that drives constant challenge and growth. I have to constantly be on the edge.

By pivoting my life around delivering value to others, I don't make any room for egocentrism. By filling your life with alignment, you don't leave space for misalignment. This is why it is so important to establish disciplined structure within your life that opposes misalignment and supports alignment. Your Heart will learn these new ways in time, and will grow into new, aligned patterns, which will, in turn, produce extraordinary capacity to accomplish your fundamental Mission, your Original Purpose. And blessings will chase you down and overtake you.

I hope you are starting to see how fundamentally different and extraordinary this manifesto is. It is a way of life, a modus operandi. By pursuing selfish interests, you sacrifice your true Identity on the altar of egocentrism; by sacrificing yourself for your mission, you gain yourself transcendently. Understand who you were designed to be and then build up structures that align with that, even when your patterns of Desire flow hard against it. Hold true to what you know is right, and your Heart will align. I've intentionally said this twice now. It is of vital importance in the application of these truths. Knowing it is not enough. Your Heart must be brought into alignment with the Truth.

> I see real sacrifice happen daily at Classy Llama Studios, as team members choose to grow our capacity to serve instead of taking fat paychecks. Regularly, Llamas go to great lengths to juggle family and work commitments, often times giving up sleep in the process. And it's not because they're going to get crazy rich from it. It's just an extension of who they are.

We care about our community, not because of what our community can do for us, but for what we can do for our community, again, as an extension of who we are. We look for opportunities to contribute rather than take, to give rather than receive, always with the long-term intention of expanding our ability to contribute more deeply and broadly in the future. It is in this way that we have grown in our capacity so quickly. We like having abundance financially, but we do not define our finish line as a dollar figure. In fact, there is no finish line, but rather a never-ending expansion of contribution and service. Arrival is boring. Adventure never has to end!

EIGHT CORE VIRTUES

LEADERS OF SELF ARE OPEN, HONEST, TRANSPARENT, PASSIONATE, DISCIPLINED, PROACTIVE, HUMBLE, AND GRACIOUS.

Once you give something a name, it's official. When I started interviewing, I began to notice that I was looking for a few "core" virtues in each of the applicants. We called them the "Core Four." After some time, we realized we were looking for more than four virtues, and the number grew. It is now the "Eight Core Virtues," which are:

1. Honesty
2. Openness
3. Transparency
4. Passion
5. Discipline
6. Proactivity
7. Humility
8. Grace

The stronger you are in the Eight Virtues, the more potential you have as a leader and team player; the weaker you are in the Virtues or the fewer you possess, the less you will be a leader and the higher risk you are to a team. This clarity has been solidified through my experience of dozens of team members and applicants, not to mention seeing it play out accordingly in people in general.

CHAPTER SIXTEEN

HONESTY

One of the most common personal characteristics listed on resumes and applications is "honest." It's even present in the old cliché, "just an honest, hardworking guy." The common understanding of the word is that it implies truthfulness, the absence of fraud, and dependability. And while this definition is good, it is incomplete, or rather, misleading. We cannot represent truth, or reality, accurately to others if we misrepresent it to ourselves. And since we all have misperceptions and misrepresentations of reality, we are dishonest to an extent according to the traditional definition of the word. But, in truth, honesty is not the state of truthfulness, but rather a condition of the Heart, a deep-seated intention.

I have met many people who drink alcohol as a sedative, an escape from reality. Their poor performance at work, at home, or at school has driven them to escapism because they have the misperception, or misrepresentation, that they are only as valuable as their performance reflects, so they seek an escape from their false reality that they are worthless due to their poor performance. According to the textbook definition, these people are very dishonest all the time because they're constantly trying to hide or escape something that isn't even true, an act that is vastly misrepresenting reality.

But I would not call these people "dishonest." I might call them confused or unhealthy or misguided, but not dishonest. They do not know the truth; therefore they are not equipped to represent it accurately. True ignorance is not dishonest.

I have come to believe that honesty is a position of the Heart, a representation of truth to the best of one's abilities, a commitment to reckon with what is. Through the dozens of people I have interviewed and/or gotten to know, I am convinced that most people are genuinely honest. That's certainly not to say that they represent the truth accurately, not even about themselves, but they represent truth to the best of their abilities, and I can't reasonably ask more than that of anyone.

However, there are those people that almost-consciously deceive themselves and others into believing something to be true that they know is not. The deepest parts of their Soul bear witness against them, though, and they are aware of their falsehood without being conscious of it. These people are not honest, but they are not expressly dishonest either. They have burned the truth out of themselves through self-deceit and therefore are no longer equipped to represent truth accurately, even if they fully intend to. I've met many "honest" salespeople who fit this description. They believe so strongly in what they are selling, and yet they omit many important pieces of information that would cause resistance in their audience. They are so out of touch with reality, so submitted to their fear and greed, that they no longer see their misrepresentations of their product or service. If confronted, many of these salespeople would defend their honor to the grave, though this is often as a result of pride and fear rather than genuine ignorance.

Simply put then, honesty does not equal truthfulness. It equals pure intent to be truthful and to reckon with reality. People that have weak intent or weak understanding of truth, however, will often end up representing a great deal of falsehood, even though they are completely honest.

That's why honesty alone is not an adequate foundation. But it is still an essential, core virtue, for if the intent to be truthful is lacking, there is no hope at all.

CHAPTER SEVENTEEN

OPENNESS

Imagine you have a stomach ulcer, and you go to a doctor and ask him for something to cure your ailment. The doctor responds by recommending the spiciest pepper in the world, the naga jolokia chili. You smile knowingly. This doctor has a good sense of humor, you think. He smiles back, clearly communicating he isn't joking. The doctor goes on to explain that the very chemical that makes any chili pepper spicy, called capsaicin, is the very same chemical that heals the stomach. Yeah, you think to yourself, that's crazy; spiciness will cure my stomach, which already feels like it's tripping on acid (and not in a good way, hippies). *Very funny*, you think. He forges on, informing you with complete seriousness that it will also prevent heat stroke. It stops being funny, and you start to get upset that you're going to be billed for this visit. He goes on to explain a bunch of mumbo jumbo medical stuff, none of which you hear because your mind is made up.

Your diagnosis is that this doctor is broken. You'd probably die from the chili pepper alone, much less from its effect on your stomach ulcer! He's asking you to consume a chili pepper five times spicier than a habañero and almost twice as potent as the next spiciest pepper in the world to prevent heat stroke. You politely tell him of his incompetence and demand a prescription for something made in a sterile laboratory, preferably something that won't melt your tongue. He relents, making a lot of money from writing the prescription, far more than he would have from prescribing the chili pepper "remedy." It's clear he doesn't understand capital gains either.

A couple years later, you point and gape when see the same guy on primetime discussing his new best-selling book of holistic treatments, including the naga jolokia treatment for stomach ulcers and prevention of heat stroke. It turns out the guy was right, and it was just too far outside of your "box" for you to accept as even possible. So who was really broken in this hypothetical situation, you xor the doctor?

Just to be clear, your "box" is measured by the length of your experience, the height of your knowledge, and the depth of your understanding *(Fig 17.1)*. Like most people do, you probably tend to identify any new experience that doesn't fit within the volume

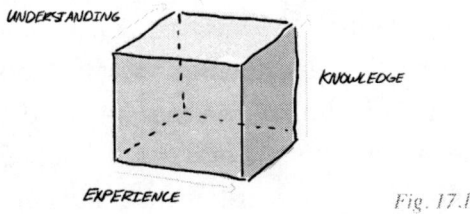

Fig. 17.1

of your Box as being impossible or incredible. It's very easy to become comfortably enveloped by your Box, to get to a point where you feel you've learned enough, experienced enough, and understood enough to stop.

But you really need a constant flow of disruptive ideas. A disruptive idea is any idea that, if true, conflicts with your current understanding of reality. The more it conflicts, the more disruptive it is. I tell the hot chili story to underscore a very common reaction that people have to disruptive ideas. We usually omit them at the onset without giving them a chance to ring true; not only would the disruption be too painful if it were true, but the time and effort it takes to consider disruptive ideas seems counterproductive to many. We do this with business, relationships, and our understanding of our Origin. In this way, openness is the choice to objectively consider ideas and experiences that are outside of their box as genuine possibilities.

Fig. 17.2

Openness also has a second, slightly different definition and application. Openness is the choice to receive and give constructive criticism and suggestions for improvement, which requires one to identify the imperfection and then to present the solution, respectively *(Fig 17.2)*. This is critical (no pun intended) to the quality of individual and team dynamics. For most, it's actually more difficult to go out of their way to give criticisms and suggestions, not only due to the inconvenience factor, but also from the fear factor. There is so much fear associated with presenting someone with a better way of doing things because you can't control the reaction. What will they say? Will they get mad at me? Will they reject me? Will it cause resentment between us? You're trying to help them, and they slap you in the face for it! As Donnie Darko would say, "Fuh-get about it." It quickly becomes something that isn't worth the effort. You decide it's sticking your nose where it doesn't belong, so you keep it to yourself, even though it's *really* bugging you.

But if the recipient isn't inviting suggestions for improvement, it actually is sticking your nose where it doesn't belong; constructive criticism is usually one of those things that must be invited to be effective. The leaders on our team make it publicly known that we are not just open to suggestion, we passionately seek it. Can you imagine upper-level leadership openly asking for someone to tell them where their performance is off the mark and how they can improve it? Imagine how much they would learn. For most team leaders implementing this for the first time, it would probably be like clamping their mouths on the end of a garden hose as years of unreleased pressure from their staff came roaring at them. It's really a funny picture when you think about it. Someone in your office should Photoshop that very image of your boss with the caption "We dare you!" and display it publicly.

I presented a marketing plan to my web development team recently, and in the fifteen-minute conversation we had about it, the plan changed significantly as my idea of quality was challenged by everyone else. We had a very specialized audience to reach; there were only 6-10 businesses that fit our target description. I realized that with such a small market, we could afford to be very personal and surgical with our marketing. I presented the plan to research each business, get familiar with the leadership rhetorically, and then send personal letters to the business leadership of each company every other week until we receive a response from them for up to fifteen letters. So the proper preparatory research was there, the surgical, targeted message was there, and the persistent repetition was there. Perfect, right?

Wrong. Before I explain, please keep in mind that these are primarily programmers by trade, so they shouldn't have anything to contribute to a marketing discussion, right? Wrong, again. First, someone mentioned that we just needed to find out if the target audience had a need for our service, so they suggested calling the company after the first letter was sent instead of pestering them to death with a thousand letters. It wasn't the most novel concept ever, but unquestionably a much faster, less time-intensive, and more effective approach. Considering how ridiculous my plan looked after this suggestion, I must admit my pride rose up and wanted to resist it, or at least make it look like that was part of my original plan, but I reined in my urge to protect my ego and accepted the recommendation in humility. And I was humiliated since I'm supposed to know what I'm doing in the marketing department, not some scab from programming! Other suggestions were made and the plan grew into a team-approved quality product. We progressed from a multi-month, man-hour-intensive, client-irritating approach to a two-week, relatively time-cheap, client-respecting approach. Bad day for my ego; good day for the team; good day for our potential clients; and ultimately, a great day for me.

But this isn't just for top-level leadership. Team leaders just set the bar for the rest of the team; as they say, "Change starts at the top," which I agree with in most cases, though it's becoming less true all the time, a trend I support wholeheartedly. But if you, as a leader at any level, adopted this approach yourself and invited and sought out constructive criticisms and suggestions, you would experience so much friction, you would either have to stop asking for it, or yield and grow, and by doing so, you will actually create the space for others to be open as well *(Fig 17.3)*. But that's terrifying for most people. They lack the self-confidence and have too poor of an evaluation of themselves to do this. Instead of responding to friction with productive action, they respond with defensiveness or self-defacement.

Fig. 17.3

I was just chatting with an individual over Skype about his business, and as I asked difficult questions about it and made constructive suggestions about how I thought he could improve his business, I could sense the tightening line of defense, and I realized that he really didn't want to hear what I was saying. So I bowed out of the conversation. This is exactly the kind of reaction we fear and the reason we don't want to give or receive constructive criticisms or suggestions. We are afraid of the reaction from the recipients, and we are afraid of what it means about our value to receive it because we attach our personal value to our performance, and we have a false image to protect.

To be fair, though, to a certain extent, the fear of negative response, be it unnecessary, is not unfounded. There are many dull blades out there whose pride will not suffer anyone pointing out the burrs and chinks that are causing them to be less effective. It's like gold refusing to be churned in the refinement process. If it refuses the fire's softening effect, its impurities will never rise to the surface and be exposed for removal. Ultimately, I'm now getting ahead of myself and talking about the vice opposite Virtue #7. Pride is the killer of progress and goodness in general, and that holds can be seen in its repulsion for criticism as well.

But the sad reality is that if everybody clams up out of fear and refuses to make suggestions, you lose untold value from the loss of "iron sharpening iron." The iron blades just stay away from each other to avoid the friction. And we lose countless hours and countless degrees in quality of life because we're too afraid of making some sparks fly.

Imagine for a moment, though, if we actually accomplished what we think we want: A friction-free environment; nothing to slow us down, change our direction... it sounds like bliss, right? But what really happens in a frictionless environment? Look at the moon. Does it look like it has had a tranquil life to you? Not even remotely. The truth is, if we got what we thought we wanted, we would be dashed against other fiercely sharp and jagged people that haven't been smoothed by the waters of life. It's an image of terrible violence and destruction. Compare that with the river bottom, where rocks smoothed from millennia of friction rest peacefully together in the midst of the most violent rapids. We want the peaceful, well-rounded life, but we are unwilling to pay the price. Ironically, progress requires resistance.

CHAPTER EIGHTEEN

TRANSPARENCY

At its core, transparency is allowing others to see all parts of a person or business, including the weaknesses, ugliness, and embarrassing filth. Without transparency, suggestions for improvement are much less likely as it is more difficult to see those things that are lacking or imperfect. I've presented this concept to many team leaders and members, and the response is fearful negativity with a measure of open-mindedness from a few. Most teams don't have very rigorous personal criteria for new team members, so I can understand why they expect a negative result of such a transparent approach. They're probably right.

But in reality, these team members are evaluating some or all of their team as untrustworthy. Any time a person resists transparency, it is due to lack of trust. It can mean one or both of two things: They are inordinately untrusting and/or some on the team are genuinely untrustworthy with that kind of information and therefore create an unsafe environment for transparency.

Individual Transparency

We, as humans, typically live life hiding, either behind our false image that we want others to believe is who we really are or through simply seeking to remain unseen. Some of us present a confident, competent, fearless image to the world; others present mere opacity. We don't want people to see what we fear about ourselves, that we are inadequate, unlovely, and worthless, or that we really just want to serve our own interests despite the burden it imposes on others. It seems most people fall into one of two camps: Those that seek to be worshiped and served by others, and those that seek merely to survive. In either case, we act egocentrically.

What's important about both modes of operation is that they are based on hiding. As we hide behind our veils, we see what we desire for ourselves in others: confidence, contentment, and self-worth. We grow to resent those who look like they have what we want, so we hang on to any little proof we can that they are faking it, and we stockpile them in our Soul's treasury and use them as weapons to tear down the resented individuals to prove to the world and to ourselves that they are frauds, which is why so many enjoy reading about celebrity divorce and drug abuse. But in these actions, we actually testify to our own lack of confidence, discontent, and feelings of worthlessness because if we had all that we wanted, we would find no pleasure in tearing others down.

It is a game of balance between tearing others down and promoting Self's image. The game is more commonly known as politics, the manipulation of the appearance of Self and others to the greatest advantage of Self. This is true of politics on the highest levels of governmental elections to the lowest levels of cubicle madness and children at play. It's all the same horrible, dehumanizing game, and it never accomplishes any good. Some are better at playing this game than others, but all humans play it in some respect. Consider: How does politics affect your everyday life? How do you engage in politics? Cut these things out of your life and replace them with openness, honesty, and transparency.

What is important to note though, is that politics generates a natural state of distrust and division within team settings. Politics is one of the greatest contributors of inefficiency and counter-productivity in every context, be it business, governmental, family, or playground. It takes potential energy for productivity and uses it for the counter-productive measure of misrepresenting the appearance of Self and others in a way that seems advantageous to Self. But in truth, if everyone stopped engaging in politics, and instead focused their energy on living according to their Original Design abundantly, everyone would be advantaged to a far greater degree than they could in seeking their own advantage. But because we don't trust everyone else to adopt this mode of operation, we don't adopt it either, as so many have the paralyzing belief that if they're only one being transparent, they get screwed.

Transparency is the diametric nemesis of politics. Increase one to decrease the other. If everyone's weaknesses are known to everyone else, striving to manipulate appearance and perception is completely moot. Hiding is impossible; politics are obliterated. It has to start somewhere, though. It has to start with a single person stepping up to the plate and leading others away from politics and into transparency *(Fig 18.1)*. For teams, this is where leadership

Fig. 18.1

comes into play. Individual transparency is impossible to regulate and police. You cannot force individuals to reveal their weaknesses, fears, vices, desires, pain, hope, talents, faith, and all the other elements within us that we choose to hide away from others. There is no official "deployment" of individual transparency. It can only be cultivated by example and invitation, and it requires leaders to take that first step and become transparent themselves, setting the example for others and inviting trust and vulnerability from others as well*.

If this sounds risky to you, that's because it is. Transparency is the state of vulnerability, and vulnerability generates friction. Your team may or may not stand up to such friction. It's likely that at least parts of your team will lose constitution and implode under the pressure. If you, as the team leader, hold true through the process, though, the team will shed the chaff and retain the gold. If you have a lot of chaff on the team, it will cause a lot of attrition. Introducing healthy friction into the team is a great way to refine it. The greatest danger is in stopping halfway through the process, and the process is very painful, so the temptation to give up will be readily available. Once you start, though, there's no going back.

---

*   If you desire to live transparently, but you are on a team whose leadership embraces confidentiality and political tension, I would recommend you earnestly seek an alternative team that will invite and cultivate your transparency. It's not easy to find, but it's worth the effort.

But if you are able to hold through the dark times of refinement, you will emerge with a team that trusts itself, a team that is comfortable being honest, open, and transparent, and it will reap all the benefits of having these qualities. It will likely take a significant turnover to get there. As Jim Collins says in Good to Great, the very first step of turning a good company into a great company is to get the wrong people off the bus, the right people on the bus, and to put the right people in the right seats. It's not vision or motivation or business plan; it's the people on the team and how they operate within the team. I cannot stress enough the wisdom of those words.

But please recognize that you do not need to wait until the team leader takes the first step. You are a leader. If you take the first step into transparency, you become the team leader, the one setting the example. If for no other reason, do it for your own health and growth. Let down your guard and live freely!

My Confessional

I consider openness, honesty, and transparency, jointly, to be one of the most radical ideas presented in this manifesto. It is still radical for me to embrace these virtues. And it seems the more I incorporate them, the more value I create in my life. But I have discovered some steep costs of living these virtues. A part of me is committed to appearing "put together," poised, and composed, and living these virtues consistently destroys that false image. They uncover the reality that there are many areas in which I am a mess.

To this day, I still choose not to be fully transparent, and I cover up many things that I believe will produce an unfavorable response. For instance, I try to appear wealthy in order to garner respect and honor. Am I wealthy? Not by my standards. I currently earn between $50,000 and $100,000 per year, and I have a net worth under $500,000. I own a minivan. Wealthy people don't drive Ford Windstars. I do. So if I'm meeting someone to whom I feel I need to appear wealthy, I will do my best to not let them see me getting in or out of my vehicle. And if we go together somewhere, we'll take their car, because on top of it being a Ford minivan, it's probably a mess as well, which further undermines my credibility and my image of refinement. And if we do end up taking my minivan, I'll quickly blame the mess on parenthood, which is a big, fat excuse!

And that's not all, if I feel I need to appear wealthy, I'll discuss how much revenue my company is pulling in and elaborate on the vision for our future. I am selective about what I mention. It's a dark art. I say the right things and avoid certain topics so as to present an artificially inflated image of myself for others to worship. It's a fear-driven dance. What if they know I'm not a millionaire, not even close? What if they know that I'm disorganized? What if they know my many weaknesses? I fear that "they" will no longer be interested in helping me and my business grow. I find I am still deeply engrossed in the "fake-it-'til-you-make-it" mentality, and I believe it's holding me back in a big way. I'm not being the real me. I'm being the "me" that I think others will respect enough to support.

My motivation is often what others will approve of rather than what is really good for me. I also often do things that are good for me, but for the wrong reason. For instance, I believe it is wise to carry a 3X5 card with my goals written on it and a few key reminders to keep me on course. But my current motivation to do this is because I heard a story about a guy whose mentor asked him to produce it, and when he didn't have it, the mentor was disappointed.

So I want to make sure I have it on me in case an imaginary mentor asks me to produce it. As it goes in my head, I feel very good about myself as I bask in the mentor's glowing gaze of approval. Yeah, I know, it's pretty demented. But this is the kind of stuff that goes on in my head all the time. I disown myself to get what I superficially want. That's messed up. And yet, I see so many others doing the same thing. It's a disease that spreads through people, and I am a carrier, a contagion. I choose in this moment to be true to myself, to be authentic. And my commitment to authenticity will be tested.

CHAPTER NINETEEN

PASSION AND DISCIPLINE

A question I commonly ask in interviews is, "What is your passion?" or "What are you passionate about?" I commonly ask these questions in interviews. Everyone has the ability to be passionate, and I would go so far as to say that most are passionate about something, whether it's a sport, vocation, a type of video game, ice fishing, whatever. It's pretty easy to discover what it is because people love talking about their passions. It presents itself when you're not even trying to find it.

As I've already stated, Passion is not something you choose to have with your Head. It's something your Heart generates with or without your consent. But you can guide it by feeding positive desires and cutting off negative desires. If, however, your Heart accepts certain fundamental ideas as true, it is much easier to invite it to accept more practical Passion. For example, if your Heart accepts and believes that people are intrinsically valuable, then it is relatively easy to get it to accept that serving people is good. And if it can accept that serving people is good, it can more easily accept that building a business to serve people is worth the pain and effort required to do so.

Differences in fundamental beliefs may have the same practical output in some circumstances, but they will also have vastly different practical outputs in others. For instance, while someone might come to the same conclusion that building a business that serves people is worth the pain and effort out of an egocentric belief because the profit from the business will serve their own interests, this fundamental belief would have a very different practical output if the business runs into financial difficulties and the owner has to decide whether to tell everyone right away or keep them in the dark until it can't be hidden any longer, as was the case with Enron.

Discipline is a buzzword that makes many people suddenly feel unworthy or incompetent, but that's just because it is exercised outside of its proper context. Discipline will always frustrate if it is used improperly. As I mentioned earlier, Discipline, also called Willpower, is the muscle behind Will. Discipline, as an extension of your Will, should drive the *initiation* that is in alignment with your Passion.

You've experienced this initiation a thousand times. You know how it feels to be lazing around on a Saturday afternoon, and a friend or family member suggests an outdoor activity. You know you'd enjoy it once you got up and started, but it takes a lot of effort to get yourself into motion. So you sit there and build up the Willpower and then, *bang*, you jump up and go. You and I both know that once you're up, it's much easier to keep going; it quickly becomes something you enjoy rather than something requiring effort.

I have this same issue with getting up early. When I was writing fragments of this book last year, I had been getting up at 5:30 every morning to write and read. For the first couple of mornings, it was agony to pull my deadweight out of bed, but after a few mornings, I started to experience the benefits of being up so early, and I really liked it. By about half way through the first month, it became a matter of course to get up and get going. It still wasn't easy to pull myself out of sleep at that hour, but I had a strong enough connection with how much I would enjoy the morning to make it almost effortless to get up. I confess, though, there are still some mornings where it is far from effortless, but it's always worth it, especially because I reward myself for getting up with a hot cup of Earl Grey.

I mentor a few friends on a regular basis, and recently, one of these friends was talking about how hard it was to live with himself because he knew he could perform better than he was if he was just a little bit more disciplined when, in reality, he lacked Passion. He was trying to force his way through life. Sound familiar? I told him he was fighting a losing battle. He was focused on the engine when he should be focused on the fuel.

It seems there is a False Self inside each of us that wants to be doing the opposite of what we desire. While working on a project we love, we are still drawn to all of the unproductive distractions that pass by us. Checking your online social networks, reading e-mail, watching that funny video your friend sent you the link for yesterday, checking the score of last night's game, making progress in your favorite video game or ... Fill in the blank with your life's distractions. We all have them, and they are all deeply seductive to the false Self within us.

Focus is almost just a mental check when such temptations arise that reminds us why we are doing what we are doing and realigns us with our true Desire as opposed to our "false desires," those desires that flow from our False Self. The strength of our focus is directly proportionate to how deeply it is attached to our sense of Identity and Purpose. Freedom from the oppressive persuasion of our false desires comes from a deep and clear understanding of who and why we are and a deep, Heart-level connection with that truth and how it connects with what we are doing in a given moment. It is possible and healthy to be passionate about who and why we are.

If you do not have that connection and understanding, however, it is very difficult to discern which voice is yours and which is your False Self's voice. Without a clear connection, it is very easy to get confused and choose something that is not in line with who and why you are, and it doesn't become clear until later. It's that awful feeling of regret that creeps over you as the moment of reckoning descends upon you. I remember that feeling after wasting away my day gaming for hours upon hours in my teenage years, and when I was done, I regretted my actions. But the very next day, I would be at it again. I was deeply under the influence of my false desires. And that's how it goes: The more we satisfy false desires within us, the more real and irresistible they will become. And then, the only time we are not unsatisfied is when we are satisfying those false desires. They become the master and we the slaves.

Following through is one of my primary weaknesses. I read two-thirds of a book and won't finish it. I start a business and get bored with it six months later. I commit to a speaking engagement only to feel trapped shortly after committing. I have largely conquered this issue, but the temptation to shift focus in the middle of a commitment still calls out to me on a regular basis. I have to remind myself why I made the commitment in the first place, and that it is, in fact, still a good reason for continuing in it.

It seems like the beginning and end of commitments are the most vulnerable spans of the journey, much like commercial flight. As Jim Collins describes, a flywheel at rest takes a great deal of energy to move. And after the initial static friction is overcome, it takes constant pressure to keep it accelerating. It doesn't feel like you're making much progress at first, which can be discouraging, but if you focus and persist with a strong belief that your efforts will bear fruit, eventually the flywheel stops resisting your efforts; instead, its momentum actually begins to aid your efforts.

Flywheels

Each of us has a unique flywheel. Some of us have a very heavy, broad flywheel that requires a lot of energy to get moving and a long, consistent pressure before it gains productive momentum, but once it's going, it's an unstoppable, highly productive force. The weakness of this type of flywheel, of course, is the necessary energy input to get to that point of productive momentum. Others, like me, have a light flywheel that is very easy to initiate and get to the point of productive momentum, but of course, the downside is that the productive momentum of light flywheels is easily disrupted.

It's easy for a person with a heavy flywheel to look at a person with a light flywheel and feel envious or resentful, and vice versa. Both types of people can bolster their weaknesses and develop a more well-rounded flywheel (no pun intended). But both types of flywheels are very important to have on a team. The light flywheels initiate the movement of the heavy flywheels and the heavy flywheels even out the roller coaster energy of the lighter flywheels. One type is no more important than the other. I'm always trying to develop the strengths of being a heavy flywheel while retaining my lightness, but I believe I will always need heavier flywheels on my teams to keep me grounded.

Discipline vs. Stucture

While a lack of Passion is commonly to blame for forward movement, a lack of Structure is as frequently to blame. Structure is different than Discipline. Structure is the systems, guidelines, and rules established to complete something. Discipline is how well you can operate within a Structure. So often, people blame their lack of achievement on a lack of Discipline. They say, "If I was more disciplined, I could complete this." 9 out of 10 times, I've found it actually can be sourced as a deficiency in Structure, not Discipline. The strength of your Discipline isn't really even tested in the context of limited or poor Structure.

I watch NBC show called *The Biggest Loser*, on which contestants lose weight with the support of professional trainers, a professional gym, and a professionally managed diet. Before competing on the show, these contestants were very obese and experiencing major health issues. They didn't work out. They ate junk food and they ate in gross excess. And yet, the moment they step foot on the Biggest Loser Campus, they suddenly are able to work out until they vomit, eat healthily, and lose tons of weight. The four top contestants even run a marathon after just four months of being on the show. Many of these contestants blame their weak Discipline for their obesity. The reality is that their Discipline, ability to work within Structure, wasn't lacking; they lacked the Structure that the show provides for them.

Not only will learning to build better Structures make

you more effective, but it will also give your Discipline muscle more exercise, and it will become stronger as a result. People go to the military to learn Discipline, and while they have the opportunity to build that muscle greatly, they never learn to build their own effective Structures, which is why so many of them feel lost and abandoned when they leave the military. The military provides the Structure so they don't have to.

The most successful businesspeople in the world are effective "Structurers." They produce the effective Structures within which others operate effectively. Everyone can work very effectively if they have someone else telling them exactly what they need to do. Building a Structure yourself is just like telling yourself exactly what you need to do so nobody else has to. You can do this for yourself and be successful, or you can do it for yourself and for others and be outrageously successful. In short, lack of discipline is nearly certainly not your primary weakness. Check your ability to build quality Structure.

Where have you been blaming your weak Discipline for your lack of success when you should be blaming lack of or poor Structure? Do you fear creating effective Structures within which to operate? If so, dig in and find out why you fear it. Challenge: Design a Structure to achieve a goal with specific tasks to be accomplished at specific times, a reminder system, and a rewards system and see how well you adhere to the system. It's like designing a game you'd like to play, except you make real progress and you experience real rewards. For more information on why this works, Google "game dynamics."

CHAPTER TWENTY

PROACTIVITY

The majority of people do not have a passion for overall growth. They may desire growth in a very specific phylum, such as a vocation or a sport or a skill. But when I say "passion for growth," I'm talking about a desire for growth in general, to improve as a person in every area of your life, bar none.

Passion for growth is a way of life, a deeply-set mode of operation. It affects how we think every moment of every day, and that's where proactivity comes into play.

Proactivity is a mode of thinking and acting. It is a mind that lives in questions and answers rather then closed-ended, mind-numbing statements. To understand proactivity well, it is important to contrast it with its opposite: Reactivity. The easiest way to see the difference between the two is by identifying how each mode of operation processes obstacles and failure.

When faced with an obstacle, proactive people immediately get to work identifying the nature of the obstacle and solutions for overcoming it, all through an internal dialogue of questions and answers, and possibly an external dialogue as well. They view obstacles as an opportunity to exercise their creativity and grow in strength and adeptness. While they do not enjoy every obstacle that presents itself, they know they must overcome the obstacle. They identify the nature of the obstacle, develop a solution, and execute the solution. If that solution doesn't work, they review their original process, learn from the failure, and try a different solution in light of the new information.

Reactive people hate obstacles, because obstacles pose the possibility for failure, and reactive people loathe failure and will develop a pattern of life that avoids it as much as possible, regardless of how much good they must miss out on as a result. Failure reinforces what reactive people fear, that they are worthless, inadequate, and needy. So it's not hard to believe that reactive people are oftentimes those who are so committed to proving their worth and adequacy and being self-sufficient, needing no one, and other times, they are those who give up and abide in self-loathing and engage in parasitism, choosing to be overly dependent on others and living life on crutches like government support, drugs, sports, video games, alcohol, and sex. Notice that there is nothing wrong with any of these things in their ordinate place, but they become crutches when you depend on them for survival despite a complete lack of real personal progress.

Reactive people have many different responses to obstacles. One common reactive response to obstacles is to use them as an excuse for quitting or for a lack of progress. Another common reactive response is to just push against the obstacle without considering its nature, hoping that, by luck, pushing is the correct response to pass through the obstacle. You know those toy robots that keep going forward no matter what? What happens when they hit a wall? They just keep bouncing off of it and running back into it. That's what this response looks like. Finally, a third common response from reactive people is to hate themselves for not being able to overcome the obstacle. The obstacle becomes an opportunity to reinforce their sense of inadequacy and worthlessness. Instead of viewing the obstacle as an excuse, they claim no excuse except their own inability to perform.

Most reactive people are deeply committed to an unchanging pattern of life because it's safer to do the same thing today you did yesterday; obstacles get in the way of that pattern. They may avoid, reject, and ignore obstacles for a long time, but as soon as the obstacles impose on their pattern of life unavoidably, they have to deal with it. Unfortunately, they usually deal with it by doing as little as possible to defer it just a little bit longer and get it out of the way at present, which usually just makes it worse when it resurfaces. When they get around it temporarily without dealing with the root cause of the obstacle, what they don't realize is that they are dragging the obstacle behind them, sapping their productive energy and weighing down on their lives.

We've all experienced this. If you've ever filed an extension on your taxes because you "didn't have time," took your wife on a date to smooth ruffled feathers instead of communicating about the core issue, or joked all Christmas with your family instead of facing the elephants in the room, you know what I mean. And if you've ever finally fully resolved one of those issues, you've experienced the rush of additional productive energy that was being wasted on dragging that obstacle around with you.

Do you have a laundry list of items that you avoid? You're dragging them around with you in the back of your mind. You'll never get away from them, so choose to be proactive and start facing them one by one. You will become stronger as a person as a result, and you'll have more productive energy as well.

The reason people are proactive about anything is because they have an interest in it. And just as people can be passionate in specific compartments of their life but not the whole, so also they can be compartmentally proactive as well. Ideally, the virtue of proactivity is a mode of general operation that applies to all circumstances.

So how do you become proactive? You cannot just strong-arm yourself to be proactive without a strong enough reason for exerting that effort. You may know in your Head all day long that you are designed to be creative, but if you don't connect with that design on a Heart level, it is an unsustainable pursuit. It's so easy to try to force ourselves to be exactly like we "ought" to be. But if you don't step back and focus on bringing the root of the problem into alignment (your disconnection with your Origin, Heart, and/or Head), you'll become agonizingly frustrated.

While I've discussed Original and Heart disconnection, it is worth to note that many also are disconnected from their Heads, which makes it impossible to bring the Heart into alignment with truth. In either case, the key to proactivity is to introspect and identify the internal obstacles that stand in your way instead of trying to force yourself to perform differently outwardly in a long-term context.

However, even this facing of the obstacles within is impossible without an adequate desire for being an effective, wholly aligned individual. It is truly a very difficult thing to pinpoint how this desire is born, but I believe the best way to support the birth of the desire is through non-invasive, repetitive iteration of truth to the individual and a shifting of circumstances to bring about new challenges to unveil hidden Desire. There are people that try to force truth into others' lives, and that doesn't work. That's why I say "non-invasive." I believe it starts with a choice to act against your own grain, and that single choice acts as a seed that produces other choices in alignment with it, provided you protect and nurture it, and eventually, after much tending and time, it bears fruit. And while I remain a student, I believe this initial choice precedes the felt Desire for it, so if you're waiting for a feeling, wait no longer. Your Desire will come into alignment with the structure you create around it.

I heard someone say that, in sales, there are trappers and hunters, those that wait for the business to come to them, and those that go out and find the business. I believe you are either a trapper or hunter of life as well. Either you're reactively waiting for life to come to you, or you're proactively going out and getting it. For those who trap, your focus is survival, and life cannot reach you in fullness, so stop waiting. Life comes to those who pursue it.

The "Lemming" Test

I often use what I call the "lemming test" to determine how proactive an individual is. Lemmings are animals that characterize reactivity quite well. One lemming will get a strange urge and start running in an unknown direction for no apparent reason. And for some inexplicable reason, the whole herd of lemmings follows this one leading lemming. Unfortunately, the leading lemming, though he has no idea where he is going, must feel energized by the degree of followership he has developed and so will keep running blindly in the randomly chosen direction, even if that includes running right off a cliff with the entire herd in toe (For some reason, this makes me think of Twitter). I'm not making this up. Lemmings really do exist, and they really do accidentally commit mass suicide from time to time due to blind reactivity.

Consider that everyone starts out as a child, and as children, we are rightfully dependent, being ill-equipped to provide for ourselves. We are deeply inquisitive about everything. We ask "why" about everything, frustrating even the most knowledgeable and well-rounded adults. We start out not being productive at all for lack of ability. As we grow, ideally, we become more independent while retaining our inquisitive nature, and we learn to work by parental example and leadership. This growth pattern is the path to adulthood.

Frequently, however, children's inquisitiveness is stunted, and they remain in a dependent mindset, possibly shifting to different hosts such as an employer and the government instead of their parents; others elect to remain with their parents forever. While they may or may not work hard, they have never learned to work effectively. This is the path to lemminghood.

A lemming is a child that has lost his or her inquisitiveness, courage, creativity, and commitment, and has resorted to the safety of following the herd. You need to know where you fall on the continuum between adulthood, childhood, and lemminghood and where your team members fall.

The lemming test is simple, and it provides good insight into this query. I pose a hypothetical situation to individuals and ask them how they would respond. I tell them they sit down for an interview, but instead of being interviewed, the interviewer tells them they're hired with a salary of $50,000 per year, and they'll be on trial for 30-days to determine whether or not they're worth the salary. The interviewer gives no information about the business at all. He merely says, "Justify an annual salary of $50,000 over the next 30 days, or this isn't going to work out." I then ask the applicant what they would do during that 30-day trial. To be successful in such a circumstance requires intense proactivity, so it is a great test to assess their level of proactivity. Please note that this is a compartmentalization of proactivity, but similar lemming tests can be constructed for other areas of life as well.

CHAPTER TWENTY ONE

HUMILITY VS EGO

I don't know how many times I've said this, but I'll say it again for you. Egocentrism, or the prioritization of False Self, destroys everything it touches. Ego is the opposite of Humility. In the same way that Egocentrism results in egregious destruction, Humility results in extreme productivity. Humility is the belief that other Selves are deeply valuable and worthy of your service and that you need others in order to be fully and truly yourself. If there were one thing I would want you to take away from this book, it would be that Humility is the cornerstone of quality leadership and quality of life.

When I was 17, I took a job as a server at a 1950s retro restaurant. I remember one day in particular when traffic was slow, virtually nonexistent, and one of the older servers began pulling the booths out and cleaning behind them, even cleaning the walls. She asked me to get started on a few as well. I hated that request. I didn't understand why it was necessary to clean *behind* the booths. No one even saw what was behind the booths! Of course, I did it out of obligation, but I admit I didn't do a very good job.

Certainly, the lack of quality leadership and team unity didn't do much to dispel my bad attitude. But the leadership's shortcoming did not justify my lacking. I am responsible to myself and to my Origin, so what others do should not affect my attitude and mode of operation. My Ego told me, "How dare they ask you to do this! You didn't agree to do this kind of work. You're a server, not a maid. Other restaurants would love to have you, and they would never ask you to do these menial tasks. Besides, they don't even pay you what you're worth here." Ever had a similar internal dialogue? As always, my Ego was focusing on self-sufficiency, control, and superiority.

If you think of Ego as a person that lives inside of you, it's very helpful. He is constantly trying to persuade you to protect your False Self against those around you, even those that really care for you. Ego seeks to convince you that you can be completely self-sufficient, needing nothing from anyone else. Interestingly, Ego is constantly reminding us that everyone else has their own Ego inside of them, so they are not to be trusted because they are just seeking their own private interests and don't really care about you.

If we listen to Ego and subject ourselves to his smooth words, the practical result is the isolation of the Heart. We become islands of self-focus, being concerned with our own interests and looking upon others as mere pawns in our Self-worship. Ironically, we can hate ourselves in the same step as we worship ourselves; we beat ourselves up for how weak and pathetic we are, which is an act of Self-hate, in order to punish ourselves adequately to justify our weakness, believing once again, that we can be self-sufficient, which is an act of Self-worship.

I must tell you a secret that will explain much: Your Ego hates you. He thinks you are a filthy, worthless piece of trash. He plots against you and seeks to destroy you through half-truths and manipulation. He knows your weaknesses and plays on them. He builds evidence against you at every turn, condemning you and convincing you that you must judge and justify yourself because no one else cares or is worthy or would treat you fairly.

Justification of "sin," those thoughts and actions not in alignment with who you are, can only come through punishment or achievement, though many are convinced blame works as well. Punishment is paying directly for the guilt burden. Blame is the unjustifiable reassignment of the guilt burden and therefore not true justification. And achievement is the balancing of the guilt burden. We try to perform, blame, and punish our way to justification and self-righteousness.

Many use a mix of the methods, punishing themselves with some choice words and then recommitting to performing better at the next opportunity. For some, this seems to work for a while as the performance improves, but it ultimately produces results far inferior to full potential and likely results in unhappiness. Others slide down a very deep hole of despair as they repetitively fail to perform and their commitments to future performance become feebler and feebler until they resort to Self-punishment or blame as their only means of justification.

As you judge and justify yourself, your Ego's persuasion to protect yourself from the Ego in others forces you to hide your Self-judgment. Other people become like a constant, never-ending jury from whom you must hide your many failures and ineptitudes. Those who know you and love you most are often the most dangerous because they have inside information that could destroy your defense, so you keep them at a distance. Anyone who suggests some means of improving yourself or your methods to accomplish anything becomes a threat to your Self-defense, and Ego quickly steps in to rebuff it, whether through an excuse, self-deprecation, a redirection, or an attempt to quell the "accusation" by confusing the matter.

To fight this ever-present condemnation, we hide from each other, and we futilely seek to justify ourselves through Performance and Self-punishment. Interestingly, though, we still give great credence to those from whom we are hiding. Although we stand in judgment over our Selves, we allow their judgments to affect how we judge ourselves. We begin to believe the accusations of others, even though they often aren't intending to be accusatory. We will even assume judgments based on interactions or communication we don't understand.

And because Ego, who believes we are trash, is guiding us, we assume the worst about what people think. One of my favorite questions when talking to someone who has made an assumption about another's accusation is, "How do you know they feel that way? Did you ask them about it?" We do not dare ask, because in the asking, we are acknowledging that it would matter to us what they think about us, and that is directly counterproductive to the image of self-sufficiency we are building for all to see. If they see that we do need others and care about what others think, the whole ruse goes up in smoke and our painstakingly carved image of self-sufficiency crumbles into dust before them. So, in the spirit of protecting our False Selves, we merely assume the worst so as to best defend against it.

It will be easier for those of you who have chosen to justify yourselves primarily through Self-punishment to accept that Ego has convinced you that you are worthless. But for those who are struggling to achieve Self-righteousness through performance, you will not be able to accept that truth as easily. You're so fixated on your image of proof that you've fooled even yourself into believing your own Self-sufficiency. You've kept the secret so long and lied to protect it to such length, you may not even remember what the secret is. But there is always the doubt within you, however well you have shut it up; it remains quietly but consistently. That's why you don't like sitting still; that's when you can hear it best. You always have to be doing something to avoid the quiet voice of Self-doubt. You need not be so afraid of it; all it is telling you is that you need something more than what you have, that you aren't self-sufficient and you aren't in control. It may be scary, but you are living a lie right now. You are not in control, and you need.

Many people, when they come face-to-face with this reality, shrink back and knowingly re-immerse themselves in their "Matrix," their false fantasy world, because they'd prefer to live a life couched in a comfortable lie than to live uncomfortably in truth. Consider that they've spent all of their lives convincing their tribe, their friends, colleagues, and family, that the image they've created is really them and that they are worthy of worship. It's as if they are high shaman in the tribe, the one who has been performing all the rights and proselytizing the rest of the tribe to worship this carved image, suddenly realizes that the image is a false god, made of stone by man's hand and nothing more, and the supposed deity it represents is a mere mortal, deeply flawed and broken. The high shaman has two choices: 1. Come clean and look like a fool, losing all power and influence in the tribe, or 2. Step back into the fantasy and tell no one. I've seen many people have to make that choice both ways. It's sad to see the opportunity to step into reality slip past someone unexploited. But so many people are more committed to their comfort than being true to themselves.

CHAPTER TWENTY TWO

THE PATH OF FOOLS

In one sense, everyone must be a fool who travels down the path of Self-exposure. It's like the Wizard of Oz, in all his power and authority, choosing to step out from behind his curtain and be exposed for the fake he is. Everything he worked for and built for himself is gone, and he's left with nothing. At the same time, there is likely a sense of relief that accompanies the grief as he is no longer required to maintain the façade.

This decision is universal. You must make this choice. Naturally, once you choose a course of operation, it is typically easier to continue in that course than to change courses, even if you're headed in the wrong direction. Only when great obstacles present themselves in your path does changing course become easier. Be thankful for obstacles as they offer you an opportunity to consider where your current path is taking you and if it makes sense to continue down it.

If you make that course-changing decision to destroy the image and stand before your tribe as your humble Self, you have made a choice that leads to painful, fruit-bearing growth. But just as a vinedresser keeps a grapevine from bearing fruit by cutting off its branches for two to three years in order to prepare it to bear much fruit, so the journey is often long and hard before you see the fruit of your change in course. Just as Neo in the movie The Matrix finds himself weak and pathetic upon exiting the Matrix, realizing he's never used his eyes or muscles, so you will find yourself ill-equipped to face the world transparently. All the tools and weapons you've become skilled with are foreign in this new world, and your knowledge is useless. You must learn new skills and develop muscles you've never used before to equip yourself, a process that requires the pain and tedium of trial and error; fail, review, learn, re-try. Over and over and over again. As you may or may not know, it's a painful process.

Humility is also like a person, and he is the voice in your head that responds to Ego. Where Ego speaks half-truths and deceit, Humility speaks pure truth. He is constantly persuading you of the truth that you need to trust those who are trustworthy and be transparent, exposing your ugliness to them. In doing this, he encourages real depth in relationships. He also reminds you that you are needy and intrinsically designed to be dependent.

If you submit to Humility, you open up the possibility of real, deep connection with other people and experiencing your True Self in a way that is only possible through connection with others. Through Humility, we are able to love ourselves, knowing that our imperfection does not make us unlovable or unacceptable. Rather, by loving and accepting others in their ugliness, you prove your own worth. Humility withholds Self-punishment and instead turns to Self-correction or receiving correction from others, which is merely getting back on track rather than trying to justify the imperfection through punishment. Essentially, what I'm talking about now is the Eighth Core Virtue…

CHAPTER TWENTY THREE

GRACE

Humility loves you and seeks to protect you from the death that Ego breeds. He is always looking for opportunities for quality support and guidance, looking to every person, activity, experience, and circumstance as an opportunity to learn and grow. He does not collect evidence against you; he does not require retort for justification. He promotes justification by Grace, or Forgiveness, absorbing the damage, or tort, caused by your own or another's imperfection rather than trying to make it right through retort, or a punishment equivalent to the offense directed back at the offender. You experience the pain caused by the damage without requiring the offender receive payback.

Whereas justification through Punishment and Achievement cannot be sustained, justification by Grace is sustainable because it encompasses our imperfect natures and weaknesses. It is critical that you understand that Grace is the only perfect way to justify Self. Punishment and Achievement don't work because there is no way to undo past failures through them; what's done is done. You are imperfect because of past failures; that will never change through

Punishment and Achievement in the future. And blame does not justify your sins but simply seeks to cover over them so others cannot see. Grace is the only means by which you can let go of past failures, no longer being held accountable for them.

Humility does not need to hide Self from the view of others because Grace is present and justifies the imperfection within, making Self, through Grace, paradoxically perfect and fit for full-view presentation. I cannot express deeply enough how overwhelming this truth is in practical output. If you don't have to hide anymore, you can experience deep, intimate relationships with others sustainably. Whether those who are dear to you are equipped will determine whether you can experience such a quality relationship with them, but if you are equipped, you will naturally find others who are equipped also.

The question still remains, though: Is your Self-forgiveness sufficient to justify you? As I've stated before, imperfection is the state of being out of alignment with your Origin. If there is no Original Design, and Chance is your Origin, imperfection does not exist (because chaos is the alignment with Chance). So, in truth, Self-forgiveness is very important, but it is not sufficient. If you are out of alignment with your Original Design, you are out of alignment with your Origin, and you then need forgiveness and Grace flowing from your Origin for your lack of alignment. Hopefully, your Origin is able to forgive you and is ready and willing to do so, but I will not seek to define that for you. I believe your Origin is, but that's all part of your discovery process.

Most people, those who seek to be justified by Punishment and Performance, can only live with themselves in a fantasy world of untruth. Those who are justified by Grace can accept themselves without fantasy.

Grace isn't all good news, though. To accept Grace as justification requires that you also accept that it isn't within your power to obtain justification for yourself. You need help. The cost of Grace is your Ego, to accept the reality that nothing you do will ever be sufficient to make up for your imperfection. You are inadequate to be independently perfect. All you have in your fantasy is falsely-derived power and worth, like the Wizard of Oz. Real and extraordinary power and worth is available through Humility as you are forced to turn away from your Self as the source and turn to your Origin.

Saved by Grace

Grace is the most recent addition to the Core Virtues. It plays such a crucial role in my life, and I know it does in the lives of other effective people as well. You might have heard of the Christian notion of being forgiven by the Creator. That truth has made all the difference in my life. If my Creator has forgiven me and is in a position of approval toward me, how can I righteously hold myself accountable for things for which my Origin has forgiven me? I know there's a part of me that doesn't want His help. I want to be perfect on my own strength, which is a futile pursuit, I know. But my Heart often doesn't feel what I know, so what I know can quickly become practically irrelevant.

This is why I'm addicted to approval from others. I am setting up others as my fill-in "origins," or gods. I need the gods I create in my life to approve of me. So I will do everything in my power to get that approval: Manipulate them, lie, present a false image of myself to them, coerce them, strong-arm them, blackmail them, deceive them, trade with them… the list of tactics is too long to name them all. But if I feel like I'm lacking approval, I'll do what it takes to get it. And if I'm all alone, my only option is to punish myself. I become more aware of my internal processes and events when I'm alone. All of my fear, self-doubt, self-hate, bitterness, and resentment come out to torture me.

I am very thankful I have an alternative. The pursuit of approval from false gods I create in my life is energy-sapping and ultimately futile. As I've said before, by definition there is only one true Origin, and I believe my Origin loves and accepts me as I am, and that's an incredible truth to live from. While I still often abuse myself with punishment and seek to fill my need for approval via false gods, I am free not to. I can love and accept myself as I am without external approval and punishment and even self-punishment.

One of my favorite Scriptures says, "For it is by grace you have been saved," (speaking about Origin's grace) – "through faith" (because I believe it though I cannot see it) – "and this not of yourselves, it is the gift of God – not by works, so that no man can boast." (I'm saved by grace, not by what I do or how well I do it.) For years, I sought to prove myself to get approval. Now I realize that the more fully I can accept the Grace offered to me by my Origin, the freer I am simply to be me. And that's an incredible deal. I can't even express the joy I feel being free to be me. It might sound crazy that I would step out of that position of full acceptance, but I am still entangled in my addiction to approval from others, and I still seek to justify myself independently from my Origin, because I have the competing commitment to be self-righteous, to be perfect in and of myself apart from anyone or anything else, a most futile and genuinely impossible endeavor.

The Etymology of "Approve"

I'm a big fan of words, and I'm an even bigger fan of etymology, the history and origin of words. I believe that the richest meaning of words requires a reaching back to identify their origin… just like I believe about humans, actually.

I decided to look up the etymology of "approve," because I wanted to know what its connection with "prove" was. I consider what I discovered to be truly profound.

"Approve" most recently comes from the mid-14th century French root "aprover," which means "to attest something with authority." It also comes from the more ancient Latin root "approbare," which means "to assent to as good, or regard as good."

I was right to think there was a connection between "approve" and "prove." "Prove" is the English root of the word "approve." I discovered that it is a very deep and ancient word. It can be dated to the 11th century through the French word "prover," which is rooted in the Latin "probare," which means "to test, prove worthy."

"Probare" is rooted in the (more ancient) Latin word "probus," which means "worthy, good, upright, virtuous." But it doesn't stop there. Even that word has a more ancient root from the Proto-Indo-European language, the oldest language on record, believed to be at least 5,500 years old. It's so old, in fact, that it lacks a spelling or the spelling is unknown; it only has a pronunciation: "probhwo," which means "being in front." This word, even, is rooted in two bases: The base "per" and the base "bhu," which simply means "to be."*

---

    * http://www.etymonline.com/index.php?term=approve. http://www.etymonline.com/index.php?term=prove

I know that's a lengthy path to trek, but I think it yields huge dividends. It certainly touched me to think that as I was seeking to prove myself worthy, I was really seeking to "be in front," to be presentable enough to let my True Self out and visible for all to see. I was actually getting approval for someone I was not, which made me even more isolated and less "in front." But when I connect with and stand boldly in my true Identity, and my true Original position of approval, I am able just "to be." And in that position, I am free to "be in front," I am "worthy, good, upright, and virtuous," I am "assented to as good," and my Origin "attests to my worth with authority." I am approved.

That's too deep and rich for me to digest all at once.

THE THINGS THAT BIND US

CHAPTER TWENTY FOUR

FEAR

Fear is the cause of all feelings of insecurity. You can legitimately be insecure, or not safe, but it is only a measure of your disconnection from your Origin. Insofar as you are disconnected from and out-of-touch with your Origin, you are insecure; likewise, insofar as you are connected to your Origin, you are secure.

Fear has been used to motivate and control people throughout human history. It often occurs by an ultimatum, whether implicit or explicit. "Serve me or die," "Give me all your money or I'll shoot you," "Put the gun down, or she dies," "If you lie, then your tongue will be cut out," "repent or burn forever and ever." Consider how many if-then statements and either-or statements of fear-based ultimatums you have floating around in your head. They're so deeply ingrained that you won't even notice most of them unless you have a very keen ability to introspect and a very good understanding of what to look for.

There isn't always an ultimatum attached to a Fear. That's just the means by which people coerce others through Fear. There is no end to the possible objects of Fear. Some are ridiculous in most eyes, like the fear of balloons (aka "globophobia"), some are virtually universal, like the Fear of death.

To understand Fear better, think of it like an entity whose sole mission is to dominate and control people. He seeks to paralyze you, block you from progress, and possibly even use you as a puppet to control other humans through you. He does this by first winning your trust as an advisor and then uses that trust insidiously.

Fear's opponent is Wisdom, whom I would also recommend you think of as an entity that also seeks to win your trust as an advisor but for your ultimate good rather than your ultimate destruction. There are two types of Wisdom: Experiential wisdom and spiritual wisdom.

Experiential wisdom is what most people are accustomed to thinking about when they hear the word "wisdom." Experiential wisdom is the confidence that flows from years of seasoning, so when you experience a new variation in the field of one of your core competencies, your backlog of experience quickly quells any fear you might have and recognizes the new challenge for what it is: Conquerable. If, however, the new variation extends far outside of your previous experience, your experiential wisdom will not be able to protect you from Fear's reach.

Imagine you are looking over the edge of a cliff. Fear will counsel you with urgency: "Step back away from the edge! You're looking at certain death! The wind might push you over. You might lose your balance and fall. See, you're getting dizzy!" Have you ever experienced the feeling of literally losing bodily control at these moments? Your Body gets weak, you perspire, you get dizzy, and you may even feel faint. Fear will point to these things and say, "See! You're liable to fall off. You're too weak to handle looking over the edge of a cliff! Now step away before you fall off."

What you probably don't realize is that as Fear gains an audience with you as you choose to listen to him, whether consciously or habitually, he gains increments of control over you, including your Body. It is actually Fear that is causing these physical symptoms to occur, and then he uses them to persuade you to follow him. He is wile and crafty and must be dealt with directly and forcefully to overcome.

As you step up to the edge of the cliff, there is also a still, quiet voice inside of you that is communicating something quite different from Fear. Wisdom will be just as sure to communicate the danger of the cliff to you, but it will not be in an urgent, desperate tone. It will be still, confident, and grounded. Wisdom might say, "Be aware of the wind. Stay close to the ground. Don't let Fear steal away this beautiful view from you."

Fear hates the influence of Wisdom because she (Wisdom) destroys the power of Fear through Truth. She demystifies and tears down Fear's illusions of impending demise and puts reality into its ordinate context. Fear will scream if that's what it takes to overcome the consistent, calm voice of Wisdom. But at other times, in areas where he already has control over you, he will speak in a calm, controlled voice and may even disguise himself as Wisdom.

Experiential Wisdom can only speak insofar as you have experience and understanding within that experience. She cannot help you when you step outside of your box to where you haven't been before. By default, Fear reigns supreme in the unknown areas. The phrase "fear of the unknown" is misleading, I think. It should be "Fear's unknown." It is a territory that belongs to him. If you venture there, he will meet you and either seek to block you or give you permission to enter but only on his terms. This is where you need Wisdom from outside yourself, either from another person who has experiential wisdom or through spiritual wisdom.

Spiritual wisdom flows from your Origin, so if you are not connected to your Origin, you will not be able to access this type of wisdom independently. You will need to obtain it via an outside vessel. There may be other spiritual flows within you that represent themselves as true wisdom, but they are always counterfeit.

I would say that most people don't genuinely believe that spiritual wisdom is even real. So the typical course is to find someone else who has experiential wisdom and gain wisdom from them in order to step out into unknown territory without having to submit to Fear. But at some point many generations back, experience of "the unknown" was originally gained through Fear, trial-and-error, or Spiritual Wisdom, so beware lest the "experiential" sources of wisdom you depend on are rooted in Fear.

Just to make sure we're on the same page, Fear is never, ever, ever in alignment with your Origin. It is rooted in falsehood and uses falsehood as a device through which to control you. It reaches out through your Heart to control your Head. It is not rational, ever. Anyone that says there is such a thing as "ordinate fear" simply does not understand what Fear really is. Essentially, what I'm saying is: Be courageous, for Fear is a liar and completely impotent unless you yield your power to him.

One final note. If you are a worthy vessel, Fear may seek to use you to gain control over others. He will teach you how to wield his power to control others, and as you gain control over others through Fear, you will be building a kingdom for Fear, not yourself. Fear will inevitably betray you once he has spent your usefulness. So a word of caution: If you use Fear's power to manage or control others, be aware that you are a pawn. I can prove it to you. Try changing your tune and dispelling the fear you've created; you will be faced with incredible opposition as Fear seeks to hang on to what he has won through you.

CHAPTER TWENTY FIVE

GREED

LEADERS OPPOSE GREED'S INFLUENCE.

You probably most commonly associate the word "greed" with money, but that association is far too limited. Greed is yet another "entity" that seeks to control you and leverage you for his bidding. He tempts you to Desire more than is ordinate and to pervert the direction of your desire. Whereas Fear attempts to control primarily through repugnance and derision*, Greed seeks to control through seduction and addiction. You can be greedy for food, money, sex, attention, freedom, and a multitude of other things. Greed leverages your egocentrism and your insecurity to drive you to unsustainable places in which you must subject yourself to him. He is the master behind addiction.

In the beginning of any dance with Desire, you are in control, like a man and a woman doing the tango. But as the dance continues and Greed promotes greater and greater levels of Desire, you begin to lose control. The most poignant portrayal of Greed's strategy I've read is represented in C.S. Lewis' The Lion, the Witch, and the

---

* That which repels

Wardrobe. In the book, the character Edmund is fed Turkish Delight, a form of chocolate, by the witch. As Edmund begins to eat it, he desires more, and the witch feeds him more and more and more, not limiting his intake whatsoever so as to increase his Desire for it and develop a dependency in him. Suddenly, she stops feeding him Turkish Delight and demands he betray his friends in exchange for more. Because he is so needy for Turkish Delight, he gives in and betrays them, only to then be thrown into a jail cell to rot. Edmund becomes an addict to Turkish Delight, just as we become addicted to objects of desire.

Edmund's unfortunate situation, like the development of any binding addiction, consists of clearly defined stages. If Greed chooses to try to inflame the magnitude of an otherwise ordinate desire, the process takes the following course…

The Eight Stages of Addiction

STAGE ONE: YOU ARE ORDINATELY SATISFIED
The ordinate desire is first felt and satisfied, and this is good and right.

STAGE TWO: GREED INVITES YOU TO "OVER-SATISFY"
Greed takes action and invites you to "oversatisfy" that desire beyond ordinate satisfaction. This is especially easy to observe with food. There is a point at which you are "full" and adequately nourished, but then Greed steps in and invites you to taste the delicious food beyond the ordinate point of satisfaction.

STAGE THREE: EXPERIENCING THE BENEFITS OF OVER-SATISFACTION

You submit to the temptation and experience the benefits of the over-satisfaction.

STAGE FOUR: OVER-SATISFACTION BECOMES A HABIT AND THE DEMAND GROWS

After this initial submission, it quickly becomes second-nature, and you form a habit of over-satisfying the desire. As you over-satisfy it, it naturally grows continually as any appetite will, requiring more and more to over-satisfy it, while giving you more and more capacity to enjoy the benefits of the desire's satisfaction.

STAGE FIVE: GREED TAKES CONTROL

Like adding sugar to bacteria, your over-satisfaction grows your demand at an exponential rate to an unsustainable level. In order to experience the same degree of enjoyment requires exponentially more of the object of your Desire. Greed leverages your unsustainable need for more to gain control over you.

STAGE SIX: SURVIVAL BECOMES THE GOAL

At some point as the disease runs its natural course, you cannot manage to satisfy any more through conventional means. You become desperate, seeking other objects and sources to satisfy your bloated desire.

STAGE SEVEN: YOU BECOME A JUNKY

As the dam breaks loose, your desire becomes not only inordinate in magnitude, but direction, flowing into areas it does not ever belong for its satisfaction. You are a junky, desperately clawing and conniving for your next fix. You are a slave to Greed's every whim, bought by the price of temporary pleasure. You cannot liberate yourself now.

STAGE EIGHT: YOU EXPLODE/IMPLODE

Explosion and implosion do not always occur, but if survival becomes unfeasible, one or both is imminent. Explosion is the point at which you take extreme, drastic measures to the destruction of yourself and possibly the harm or destruction of others to satisfy your desire. Implosion is when you "burn out" because you are fully dependent on the object of your Greed for an artificial sense of life. When it dries up, your feeling of life dries up, and your internal vacuity* is fully felt.

    The earlier you identify Greed's wiles in action, the easier it is to cut him off and keep him from gaining traction in your life. Do not be fooled by the seductive attraction of his offers. They are bait on a hook. He wants to control you and ultimately destroy you, just as a virus controls a cell for its own devices and ultimately destroys it in an explosion of virulent release. Beware lest you become the wasted shreds of a former human being after Greed has had his way with them. Don't forget: You are designed to lead your Self.

---

*   Emptiness

CHAPTER TWENTY SIX

LEADERS ARE SELFLESS

Leadership is frequently abused. We are all aware of the stories of business leaders laying off thousands of people to save their own skin, or cashing in on their stock days before the company implodes. And certainly, that's an abuse of leadership. But that's not what I'm talking about. I'm talking about the more common, accepted form of abuse. Every day, people get up and use their capacity for leadership to pursue their selfish interests.

In truth, this book is dangerous. It contains the information you need to understand and master your Self, and that is a power that can be used for good or evil. Unfortunately, most people use it to pursue their own selfish interests, which is most certainly evil or bad or misaligned or whatever you want to call it. You were given the capacity to lead for a Purpose, that Purpose not being to serve yourself. This is a perversion of the capacity, and in reality, it is no longer truly leadership. You cannot lead yourself toward yourself. There must be a point outside of yourself you are leading yourself toward, a mission, goal, calling, something greater than yourself.

All of the people who work their daily shift, come home and

watch TV for the rest of the evening and then go back and do the same thing again day after day after day are guilty. All the people who cut throats and compromise values to get to the top of the corporate ladder are guilty. All of the people who use other people to grow their business, not sharing in their prosperity with those that helped build it; they're guilty. The tough truth is every one of us is guilty of being selfish. The big problem is that we, as a society, have been given philosophical permission and blessing by Darwin and Smith to be selfish. Darwin gave us permission by positing that Self is the most important being in our Universe; Smith gave us blessing by positing that by living selfishly, we actually help society as well. This sick blend is what I call Darwinistic Capitalism. I hate it with all of my being (except for that ever-diminishing egocentric slice of me).

Selfishness is a disease that pollutes your entire existence. It infiltrates your worldview and permeates and perverts every circumstance you encounter and every choice you make. It doesn't actually do any good for anybody, least of all your Self. If allowed to reign within you, it pivots your whole life on the falsehood that life is about making you happy. I know what you must be thinking: "What about everything you said about being happy?!" To be clear, I did not say that your life purpose was to be happy, but that living according to your Original Design would establish happiness as a natural byproduct. Do not get confused with that being your purpose. Happiness is a blessed state of being that flows from your Origin, not something to be pursued. A good friend of mine told me that blessings overtake you from behind, so if you're chasing them, you'll never catch them. They must chase and overtake you as you live from who you really are.

I can personally vouch for this truth in my life. For the first three years of my entrepreneurial journey, I spent my time trying to pull as much as I could to my side of the table while still keeping the deal together, thinking that it was the good and proper way of the modern world. What I came to find out, though, is that by fighting for everything I could get, the "other side" was fully aware that they must pull to their side of the table or they'll end up with a bad deal. I didn't understand what it meant to do good business. I only knew how to do good-for-me business, which is largely why I failed eight times in a row.

Now, after years of painful learning, I have come to understand that by making my focus delivering abundant value to the "other side," I gain their trust, and they are more willing to pursue an equitable deal that is good for both sides. Once I stopped making it about me and started making it about delivering abundant value into the lives of others, success overtook me. Deals started closing, business started growing, and opportunities presented themselves in abundance.

CHAPTER TWENTY SEVEN

THE NEED FOR CONTROL

LEADERS DO NOT NEED CONTROL.

As a leader, you certainly must be in control of your Head and your Will. But aside from that, you have no direct control over anything else, within or without. Instead of seeking to control your own Heart and Spirit and all manner of externalities (people, objects, ideas), seek to guide, inspire, and invite productive progress. Your internal control should be able to effectively, positively react to uncontrolled externalities effectively. Some externalities must be controlled in order to accomplish a task. As a very fundamental example, if you need to dig a ditch, you must physically manipulate and control the dirt in order to sufficiently displace it in such a way so as to produce a ditch. On the other hand, people are never to be controlled. It isn't your place, or my place, or anyone else's place to control other people. I exclude children, who do need the controlling influence of their parents to guide and protect them. It suffices to simply say that it is not a reflection of who you are to seek to control others.

While it might be a simple concept to grasp that it is not our place to control others, it is quite a different matter to grasp how this same principle applies to leading Self. Trying to force your Heart into a certain pattern is about as effective as trying to force a child to poo in the toilet. Eventually, the child will learn to hate the toilet, and likewise, your Heart will learn to hate the mold into which you're trying to force it. Just as a child needs to be understood and then invited, guided, and cajoled according to that understanding, so must your Heart be.

It is a delicate art to woo your Heart. I've seen so many people who have learned to hate doing good because they've tried to force their Hearts into the deal and no matter how hard they tried, they absolutely could not beat their Heart into submission adequately, which led them to surrender to their Heart instead and cede control to it. The only sadder outcome are those that successfully beat their Heart to death and are left doing things purely according to structure (aka "the law") with no life flowing through that structure. Sad indeed.

If you're in this fight with your Heart, you must realize that your Heart is like a wild stallion. It wants to gallop on the open range. It wants to conquer and prance and snort. It wants to be free. Cage a wild stallion and see what happens. The stallion is liable to get into such a frenzy that it breaks out of the cage in a rage and kills anyone in sight. Yes, you have that kind of fierce strength within you. If you manage to keep the stallion caged, however, it will either kill itself or it will sink into despair and either starve itself to death or become a shell.

But there are other ways of forcefully dominating a horse. You can whip it when it does things you don't want it to. But eventually, you'll end up with the same outcome as the cage. Dead or beaten or both. I'm sure there have been many "horse-breakers" who feel they have accomplished their goal by beating a horse into submission. How many people feel the same way about their Heart? I don't know many horse-breakers, but I'm sad to say I know many, many Heartbreakers. People don't just do this to themselves, although they are usually their own first victim. As I said before, how you treat your own Heart is how you will treat others'.

The key challenge in this relationship is to preserve the stallion's Identity, strength, and character while harnessing it to serve you. Understand the stallion; respect it; woo it. Do the same for your Heart.

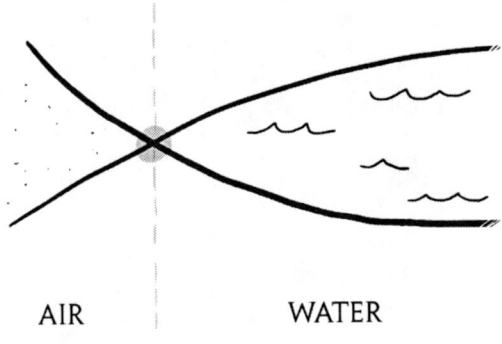

AIR   WATER

Fig. 27.1

Is it so hard to see why we are so disconnected from our Spirits? Our flowing parts scare us *(Fig 27.1)*. Our Heart is very much alive from birth, and we carelessly seek to cage it, whip it, or kill it, or we hand it the keys to our kingdom. Our Heart doesn't flow nearly as swiftly as the Spirit. As an analogy, your Heart is to water as your Spirit is to air. Water is so much easier to see, so much easier to manage, so much easier to measure, whereas air is swifter and almost dimensionless. If we have so much trouble with the Heart and the Heart starts out alive, it's easy to see how much more difficulty we have with the more intangible and complex flow of the

Spirit, especially when it starts out disconnected from its Source.

But as an encouragement, if you learn to understand, respect, and woo your Heart, you will begin to be more aware of spiritual flow. Or put another way: Swim, then fly. There's no time to learn to swim like the present.

PART FOUR
THE JOURNEY

CHAPTER TWENTY EIGHT

WOOING YOUR HEART

LISTEN, UNDERSTAND, RESPECT, ADVENTURE

I've already presented much of what you need to understand the Heart. But as you read about the Heart in Chapter 8, you probably were enlightened and enjoyed the tasty intellectual morsels I offered. And while eating tasty brain morsels is easy and fun (that came out far more Hannibal Lecter-ish than I intended), that's just understanding THE Heart. I'm challenging you to understand and connect to YOUR Heart. Truly understanding your Heart requires that you listen to it. When your mother states a thinly veiled insult about your father and your Heart rears its head in anger after years of hearing these insults, do you hush it, or do you listen to it and experience the pain it has stored up? When your wife berates you for the ninth time for not fixing the broken whatchamacallit in the utility closet, do you listen to your Heart's response? Do you hear its words of self-hatred? Or when your husband leaves you in the midst of a painful argument to escape, do you let your Heart feel the depths of its pain in your abandoned state? Of course, there's a whole other side of your Heart that is also hampered, keeping you from experiencing the heights of joy and bliss, the fervent laughter, the uninhibited regions of ecstasy. You have no idea how high or how wide you can go in either hemisphere of your Heart. It's like trying to find the edge of the universe itself. It is an adventure waiting to be frontiered.

Start the adventure. Show you Heart you really care about it. Listen to it. Give it time. Hear its deepest movements. This is how to truly understand your Heart, just like what is required to understand another person. Listen. Listen courageously. Go into the rooms of your Heart you're scared to enter. Witness the ugliness you've been avoiding. And *accept your Heart* in its ugliness because it's worthy of love.

And then, as you listen and see your Heart's depths, love and respect it enough to give it a voice. Do not be ashamed of it. Let your Heart know that you are not ashamed of it. Express it outwardly in some form. Expressing your Heart outwardly demonstrates to your Heart that you are not ashamed of it, which will build its trust in you. Be gentle with it when it is hurting. Laugh when it feels mirth. Scream when it feels excitement; weep when it despairs. If your Heart knows that you will not put it away in shame, that you will accept it no matter what it is feeling, it will trust you with more and more of itself, and the abundance that is there is limitless. Stretch as far as you can, and you will not find the edge of it. It is only once you've gained your Heart's trust that it will be willing to yield to your Head's structure and flow through it, thus giving you its incredible power.

But it isn't enough to understand your Heart, nor to merely respect it. If you do those two things, you will learn to love your Heart, and as you love it, you will want your Heart to open more and more to you. As you respect your Heart, trust will build, and that trust will make adventuring possible. This is the consummate act of wooing.

Adventuring is the act of putting your Heart in positions it has not been before, positions outside of its comfort. There it must trust you to lead it well. Beware, though, that in the same way as a stallion will spit and fight when you seek to subdue it, so will your Heart resist, even when you have established its trust. It does not resist because it doesn't desire adventure. Truly, your Heart loves to adventure; it just needs to be led boldly. And in that adventure, it grows; it expands its borders, and it gives more of itself to you. So take risks; be dangerous; and lead your Heart fearlessly through it all. Do that, and your Heart will give itself to you fully. Instead of your Heart growing from wild overconsumption, it will grow in trust-based alignment with your leadership. This is not control. It is leadership. Leaders do not need control.

A Note About Men, Women, and Relationships

Men, if you want to take a bit of a trip, re-read the beginning of this chapter, but this time, replace the word "Heart" with the word "wife," or "girlfriend," or "fiancée," whichever applies to your circumstances. Naturally, change all of the pronouns fittingly so you aren't calling your wife an "it." This might blow your mind a bit, so be prepared. Femi-Nazis won't like this, but I'll say it anyway because it's true: Women are most represented by the flowing Heart. Men are most represented by the structured, logical Head. That's not to say that men shouldn't be connected to their Hearts or that women shouldn't put their Heads in positions of leadership; it just means that natively, women are typically more connected to their Hearts and men are typically more connected to their Heads.

I honestly don't know if this is universally true, but it is densely pervasive at least.

You can apply the truths about your relationship with your Heart to your relationship with others. Romantic relationships will differ from friendships, but the fundamentals are consistent throughout.

Most importantly, in the same way as you cannot lead others until you learn to lead yourself, you cannot relate to others' Hearts until you learn to relate to your own. Start with your first relationship: Your Self.

I've Just Begun...

I feel like I've just begun my journey of building a relationship with my Heart. Even as I've written this book, I have experienced major breakthroughs in that relationship, realizing how little I was letting my Heart out to play. Actually, after reviewing the core manuscript, I realized how little I was giving my Heart a voice, so I went back through and included additional sections to remedy that. The truths contained in this book grow out from deeply personal places in me, and I believe it would be dishonoring of me to withhold those from you.

Not too long ago, I viewed my Heart from a distance, like a scientist studying a specimen. I would observe the Heart in others and learn about its inner workings. I would research with questions, go where few dare to tread in others, and in these acts of courage, I learned a great deal about the Heart. True things. But I wasn't experiencing my own Heart. Knowing is not experiencing. It was as if I was talking to people who had journeyed to a foreign land and asked them all about it. At the end of my questions and research, I had enough information to write an entire book about the foreign land, having never been there myself.

My Heart has been a foreign land to me for a long time. I'm excited to be personally exploring it now. My research of its terrain, climate, culture, governmental structure, and hot tourist attractions (sorry, analogy breakdown) has certainly served me well as I have begun this personal experience, but I have learned in no uncertain terms that experience of a thing and knowledge of it are two very different animals.

A Quick Note: Subjecting the Body

Just like your Head, your Body is a structured component through which your Spirit and Heart can flow. By establishing your Head as the leader of your Heart, your Body will be subject as well, along with its Desire for food, sleep, comfort, pleasurable sensations, and sexual stimulation. All of these things are good, but if the Body is not subjected, it will demand these things in inordinate magnitude and from inordinate objects.

In a sense, the Body is the most rigid structural member of your personhood, but Bodily Desire flows in a similar pattern to the Heart. The flow must be guided in the same way as the Heart, except your Heart's flow is necessary to guide your Body's flow effectively. In a reactive context, the outside world flows into your being and shapes your Heart's flow, but once you have the proper leadership structure in place, your Heart will flow outward, guiding and shaping the flow of your Body's Desire and the world around you.

As an example, I used to love brownies, deep-fried anything, and soda. For the most part, I detest them now. It didn't suddenly happen for me, of course, but as I learned what these things were doing to my Body and my entire personhood, I chose to stop eating them, and as I made these choices, the actual taste became abhorrent to me over time (although I admit I still crave a Cherry Coke with certain meals and must invoke Willpower to quell the craving). The Body can either block or facilitate your Spiritual and Heart flows to the physical world. If your Body is healthy, it facilitates it. If it is sick or malnourished, it will block your flows.

Unfortunately, putting toxins into your Body can also affect your Head and Heart directly. Chemical imbalances can form from improper nutrition, which lead to "mental diseases" that cripple the Head and Heart. I spoke with a woman a few weeks ago whose son developed autism after taking a vaccination that contained mercury, a relatively common result of such vaccinations. Be very careful how you treat your Body. Avoid putting toxins in your Body. It can single-handedly destroy your opportunities to grow and contribute.

Not to jump on a soapbox here, but all pharmaceuticals are, by definition, toxic; the FDA will not approve a "drug" unless you can kill animals with it at a high enough dose. Google "LD50". It'll make you think twice before taking your next pharmaceutical pill or shot.

CHAPTER TWENTY NINE

EMBRACING PAIN & DISCOMFORT

LEADERS EMBRACE PAIN AND DISCOMFORT.

Pain is an essential part of growth. If you don't believe me, go to your nearest gym and watching the bodybuilders do their thing. It's painful just to watch. They grimace and grunt and wheeze and spit. It's really quite gross, but it's also effective. They are very muscular because they have endured a great deal of pain over a long period of time, and that pain has begotten muscle growth.

There is a vast difference between growth pains and suffering. Suffering is unnecessary pain, pain that accompanies real and lasting damage to your personhood. Suffering is when we choose to abide in our pain rather than feeling it as it passes through us. Growth pain is part of a process that results in the bearing of good fruit. It accompanies progress.

Leaders embrace pain when it is necessary for growth and progress. They are unwilling to let fear of pain derail them. They will not be defeated by pain in pursuit of their mission. Like a warrior, they can be pierced, slashed, torn, broken, and beaten, but they will persevere unto death if they must.

In reality, pain is merely a warning or an alarm. It is your

Body or Heart's way of saying, "Pay attention to me! Is something wrong?" This is particularly helpful if you have your hand accidentally hanging in a fire or if you meaninglessly hurt someone else and it hurts you to see them in pain.

    It's probably more important to point out what pain does not indicate. Pain is not necessarily an indicator of danger, nor does it always indicate something bad is happening to you. Pain provides an important opportunity for you to evaluate the situation and identify the source of the pain. The source is either a vital source or a negative source. If a fire is burning your hand, you might think it's a simple matter of removing the hand. If your hand is purposelessly in the fire, then that certainly is reasonable, but if it is in the fire because you are grabbing someone out of the fire or because you must pass through the fire to make progress, it does not make sense to pull back. It is critically important to note carefully that the proper response to pain is not always to withdraw from it. Oftentimes, it is better for you to endure through it.

What walls of fire are in your path that are keeping you from making progress?

    The instinctual or conditioned reaction to pain is usually very unreasonable. When you get a headache, the common response is to take a painkiller. This is the most inordinate response possible! You have a headache because your Body is trying to make you aware of a problem. Maybe you are dehydrated. Maybe you don't have the nutrients your Body needs, either from not eating enough good food or simply not eating enough. Maybe you are excessively stressed. Maybe your spine is out of alignment. If you merely react to the headache by trying to kill the pain, you profit nothing from your Body's attempt to communicate with you. In fact, you disrespect it by not listening and trying to shut it up.

I strongly recommend that you do not ever react exclusively to pain. Instead, identify and respond to the source of the pain. If it is a sharp, unexpected pain, pulling back is recommended, but only so that you can gain perspective on the source and reevaluate. Pain is like your Body and Heart's way of shouting your name in alarm. Can you imagine what kind of relationship you would have if every time your friend shouted your name with alarm, you tell them to be quiet and tape their mouth shut? It's deeply disrespectful. It's basically saying, "I don't care if there is something wrong with you." With this attitude, is it any wonder we are in a health crisis? We aren't listening to and respecting our Bodies. What is less obvious is that we are also in a Heart crisis as well for the same reason. When our Heart hurts, we seek to medicate it with distractions like entertainment or with painkillers like sexual stimulation and drugs (including pharmaceuticals). We run away from it, or we numb it.

We do not really want to do this to our Hearts, but we do not know how to respond differently. We don't know of any alternatives. We are so quick to condemn others who are medicating their Heart conditions irresponsibly, and yet we who condemn are guilty as well. Are you aware that your Body and Heart are diseased? To cure any disease, you first need to know that you are diseased, and then you need a remedy.

The primary problem is that we prioritize comfort, and constant comfort is the surest way to learn nothing and grow not at all. It is hardship that stretches us and offers growth opportunities. We go out of our way to avoid obstacles and battles. The trouble is that by avoiding these obstacles we push ourselves deeper and deeper into a corner until eventually our entire world is reduced to the size of a pinhole. The size of that pinhole is directly related to the fullness of life you can experience in such a circumstance. By prioritizing comfort, you will quickly find yourself in uncomfortable bondage, and your life will be wasted. You are designed to be a warrior. Warriors appreciate the comfort they experience, but it is not their priority.

A Defining Decision

If I could point to one decision that defined my progress, it would be my decision to prioritize personal growth over the avoidance of pain and discomfort. I made a clear choice that I would endure whatever pain and discomfort was necessary to grow. Pain still hurt me and discomfort was still uncomfortable, but I was okay with it. In large part, pain and discomfort lost their power and influence in my life. I did not deny them; I just felt the pain and discomfort when it was present and moved past it. Feel it; keep moving forward. That has been my simple mode of operation, and it has been very effective in my life thus far. Imagine how much more effective you would be if you were not influenced by pain and discomfort. Imagine all of the things you would have done in the past that you didn't do because you avoided one or both of these obstacles. I think you will find that life can look very different if you shift your context on this matter.

CHAPTER THIRTY

YOUR RELATIONSHIP WITH YOUR SELF

LEADERS DEVELOP A STRONG RELATIONSHIP WITH THEIR SELVES.

Leading yourself effectively is made possible by a quality relationship with your Self. Just as you must first understand and respect your Heart before adventuring with it, so must you do so with your entire personhood. I've spent a lot of time explaining Self in hopes you can understand it better. This understanding makes respect possible. And by acting respectfully toward your Self, you gain the trust of your Self; trust makes adventure possible, and adventure gives way to abundant growth and life.

I know it must be odd for you to think of your Self like someone you need to develop a relationship with, but it is what it is. You need to love your Self enough to really spend the time to understand It. It's like Ralph Waldo Emerson said, "Know thyself." I would say the same thing slightly differently: "Know thy Self." You know the phrase "You just have to trust yourself." I would say: "Your Self needs to trust you, and you need to trust It." If you haven't loved your Self enough to take the time to understand It and respect It, you have no reason to expect that your Self will trust you, and if It doesn't, happiness will persistently elude you.

It's kind of like a romantic relationship with Self leading to marriage. You have to woo your Self to give all to you so you can become fully your Self. You can become one. This is what I call "Self-actualization." When you actually become one with your Self. It is our first and highest calling to actually be Self, because insofar as we are not one with Self, we are limited in relationships with others and in our ability to fulfill our Missions. In other words, if you do not understand your Self, you cannot understand others. If you do not love your Self, you cannot love others. If your Self does not trust you, nor will other people. It is the First relationship. And ultimately, it is a relationship with your Origin, because your Origin designed your Self. If you do not know your Origin, you cannot know your Self.

This marks a potential turning point in your life. Once you reconnect with your Self, a new paradigm takes effect. You are no longer at war with your Self. You have accepted Self as It is, and you are protecting It instead of hushing It, drugging It, beating It, fleeing from It, or whatever else you've done in shame for your Self. Once you realize that your Self is not defined by what you do, that it was defined from the beginning by your Origin, only then can you be free from the dehumanizing lie that you ought to be ashamed of your Self. Your Origin designed you perfectly. Shame and guilt are justified insofar as you deviate from that Original Design, but that's not you; that's a perversion of your Self. So look into your mirror and embrace your beaten, rejected, exiled, and abandoned Self. It doesn't deserve your disgust and hate. You probably treat your Self worse than anyone else.

The truth that you must love your Self and prioritize that relationship has been utterly demonized by our religious culture in the US. The religious sector tells us that loving our Selves is selfish, when in reality, we are unable to effectively love others because we've never spent the time and effort learning to first love our Selves. In fact, the presiding religious text in the US, the Bible, even says the second greatest commandment is to "love your neighbor as yourself," stated by Jesus Christ himself. So if Jesus says we are to love our "neighbor" as we love our Selves, isn't it absolutely essential that we learn to love our Selves first? That is my challenge to the overarching sentiment in the religious sector. The truth is that by taking the approach I'm suggesting, the result will be sacrificial service to others and abundant life-giving growth. It would not compromise the goal of the religious culture; it would fulfill it.

So, negativity be damned. Are you ready to step into a new life, the life you were intended to live? If so, read on. I want to show you the power it gives you and the results you can expect from leading a life aligned with your Original Design, a life aligned with who you really are.

CHAPTER THIRTY ONE

LEADERS MAKE BIG COMMITMENTS

LEADERS LEAD A LIFE OF NEVER-ENDING ADVENTURE AND CREATIVITY, DRIVEN BY STRONG COMMITMENTS.

New Year's Eve parties are a great place to experience the human capacity to make empty commitments. Making true commitments is not easy. In the common sense, commitments are just choices you make. "I will go to the store and pick up groceries" is a commitment. But words are powerful to indicate what you really mean when you think you're making a commitment. Do you use words like "probably," "possibly," "might," "maybe," "try," and other words that reduce the potency of your commitments and truly aren't even commitments? That's because you're afraid of commitments, and you're afraid of commitments because you're afraid of failure, and you're afraid of failure because you believe the lie that your performance defines you. So you play it safe, abiding in the comfortable commitment to not make any solid commitments. You're still committed; you're just committed to mediocrity and waste.

You can liberate yourself from this bondage by aligning with the Truth about who you really are. You are not defined by your performance. You are defined by your Origin. This is part of understanding your Self, and it is why it is the first step of the process. And it is very important that you overcome this belief in you, because making commitments offers two amazing opportunities:

1. To stretch and grow

2. To achieve extraordinary results.

The Anatomy of a True Commitment

Making commitments is part art, part science. I can teach you the science of it, and I can give examples of the art, but just like learning painting, it takes three ingredients: Learning technique (the science), observing other artists and their work, and practice. The art is in how you apply the science.

There are two types of commitments: Commitments to destinations within your comfort zone and commitments to destinations that fall outside of your comfort zone. Those that fall within your comfort zone do not stretch or grow you. They may bolster your confidence in your ability to perform within your comfort zone, but they will not grow your comfort zone. Only those commitments that you make to destinations outside of your comfort zone can do that, and these are the most challenging to achieve, and they are also the most powerful. I recently heard a wise person say, "Stability is an illusion. You are either growing or decaying." Dead things decay. Living things grow. I recommend you choose to live, which means you must make commitments that stretch you. The reality is if you can achieve these growth-oriented commitments, you can certainly achieve comfortable commitments.

Following are the principles of a true commitment. Think of these like the scientific laws of nature. You cannot fight against them. They just are. By abiding by the principles, you consistently achieve results according to your commit. When you step outside of the principles, you do not consistently achieve the results you commit to. It's that simple.

Principle #1: Specificity

Commitments must be made in quantifiable terms so you can measure progress and achievement. Your commitment should have a specific timeline and an achievement-oriented end. Very rarely will you want to make a lifetime commitment that has no time-oriented end. These are very dangerous commitments for the obvious reason that they never end. A good commitment statement is "I will have this book written and published on or before November 9th, 2010." It's quantifiably measurable with a clearly defined end date. I will know exactly when I have accomplished it because I'll have a published book in my hands as empirical evidence of its achievement. A bad commitment statement is "To improve my marriage." That's not even a commitment; there's no quantifiable metric by which to measure its success, and there is no end date by which you want the metric to reflect a certain value. That statement is more like a wish or a weak goal. I'm happy you desire to improve your marriage, but to be honest, your Desire is next to worthless if you don't structure it properly.

Specific commitment statements hold you accountable. They don't let you cheat or water down or lie. You either achieve what you commit to achieve within the timeframe you say you will, or you don't. Scared? That's your fear of failure and the big lie. Refer back to the first paragraph of this chapter if you've forgotten it.

Principle #2: Planning (but not too much)

You've probably been to a workshop at which people are motivated to set goals and make commitments. The next day, though, after sleep neutralizes your adrenaline, you wake up and groan at how unrealistic your goals and commitments seem. I have seen so many people make very foolish commitments at such events, and I'm guilty of it myself. The most foolish commitments revolve around money because money is just a medium of exchange. It's not really what people want. For me, money meant recognition, and that's what I was really after, which was selfish. Whether or not the commitment was wise, though, you still groan the morning after because you're quite sure you've over-committed.

To achieve the impossible requires planning. Break down your commitment into bite-size actions and schedule those actions across the time you have to complete the commitment, though I would recommend adding buffer into your schedule for unforeseen, disruptive incidents.

As an example, I made a commitment in early August to have this book written and published by November 9th, 2010. I counted the number of working days between the time I made the plan and the end date, and then I grouped milestones into a sequence, including rough manuscript completion, editing completion, cover art and graphic design completion, and publishing completion. I realized that in order to have the editing time to ensure I produced a quality book, I was going to have to get the cover art and graphic design done while still in the process of writing the manuscript. That would allow me 13 working days to edit the book, which is admittedly very scant editing time for a full-length book, and approximately two weeks for the publisher to push out the first printed book. Then, based on the book outline I created on my first day and a review of past writings, I guessed how many pages I would have to write to complete the book. I guessed 100 standard size pages (one standard size page equals about 2 print pages). I already had about 40 pages of content I could graft in from previous writing, but I still estimated I would need to write an additional 90 pages to create the rough manuscript, 50% more than I really needed to write if my estimates were accurate.

I broke those down into daily action steps, and came to the conclusion that if I wrote 2 fresh pages of content per working day (6 days per week), I would achieve that with 13 working days to spare for editing and two weeks for going to press. For intense writing like this, it usually takes me about one hour to write one unedited page, so I needed to create two hours of focused time per day on writing. If I scheduled it in the evenings, I would have all of the happenings earlier in the day to compromise the scheduled writing at the end of my day, and it also compromised my family time as well. So I chose to give up sleep to complete this commitment because I didn't have enough time otherwise. I decided to get up two hours early every work morning at six o'clock. And this is how I planned to complete the manuscript in 46 working days. By making everything so clear, I knew exactly what I had to do to make it happen, and I was committed, so I had to do it. Why did I have to do it? Because I didn't give myself any outs.

As I am conducting a final edit of this section on November 28th for a print submission on December 3rd, I am able to clearly see I missed the mark because I set a clearly defined completion date, and I have the opportunity to review the cause of the shortcoming. If I hadn't set a clearly defined commitment, I would have far less opportunity to improve upon the results with future similar commitments. Do I feel guilty and ashamed? No. I missed the mark, and I'm far from aloof about it, but I'm not ashamed. The results are out of alignment with the commitment. So, while the results are underwhelming, I look at it as an opportunity and choose to create value from it.

"Foolish Commitments"

Sometimes you have limited or no information about the journey required to achieve a result. These are particularly unnerving commitments, but they are also often the most powerful. Imagine you approach a river, and you cannot see the other side, and you have no way of knowing how wide the river is. If you commit to crossing the river by swimming, your journey consists of "one stroke at a time" for as long as it takes. You really don't even know if you have the strength to accomplish it. It creates even more pressure when you make this kind of commitment with a time commitment included. Now you must make "one stroke at a time" *as quickly as you can* or be more creative about your mode of transportation or your technique or some other aspect of the journey.

A lot of people think these kinds of commitments are foolish. Why? Because they cannot be certain of success and the risk is too great. Certainly, it is important to ensure that you're making a commitment for the right reasons, but provided that's clear, these are the most amazing kinds of commitments you can make. Bear in mind I do not speak as one above them. They scare me, too. But these are the commitments that grow us the most and make us aware of our weaknesses. And if we persevere, these commitments will also yield the most extraordinary results. You've probably heard the phrase, "Shoot for the moon. Even if you miss, you'll land among the stars," or some variation of it. While I don't think about my big commitments in this way, it's still true. If you shoot to turn $10,000 into $1,000,000 in six months and only achieve half that, you're still finishing "among the stars." Celebrate that victory *and* review to identify the cause of the shortcoming. You can do both!

Principle #3: Don't Give Yourself Any Outs

This is the single greatest reason people do not follow through with their commitments. They let their excuses excuse them. Commitments are decisions, and I mean that in the root sense of the word, coming from the Latin root *decidere*, which means "to cut off." To decide something is to cut off all other options. When Cortés made the decision to conquer Tenochtitlán, he sent one boat back to Spain to communicate with the king and "scuttled" the rest of the boats, stripping them and running them aground, making them unusable for escape. He cut off the easy choice.

Cutting off all of your options is not easy. We are very creative beings when it comes to getting out of a commitment. Here are some suggested tactics to cut off all of your options:

- Establish an environment of singular focus (take everything out of a space except what you need to focus on)

- Establish a strong positive supporting commitment if you succeed (e.g. "I will book a flight to Paris within 24 hours of succeeding.")

- Tell friends, family, and strangers what you have committed to do and the negative and positive supporting actions you will take if you fail/succeed.

- Post daily public updates of your progress on a blog or a social network or some other publication and get as many supportive people to follow you as you can.

Full commitment is one of wild abandon. Abandon all other options, and you put yourself in a do-or-die, pass-or-fail position, which is a highly effective place to be.

Principle #4: Asking for Help

More often than not, to keep a commitment requires help from others, even if that is as simple as asking for someone to hold you accountable. To complete this book, I needed the practical support of one or more artists and a printer. When you ask for support, whether it be for practicality or accountability, be specific what you want your supporters to do to help you. If you want them to contact you every morning, get their commitment to do so. If you want them to review your work once a week, ask them for that commitment. You need supporters who are just as committed to their tasks and responsibilities as you are to yours. When many people exert effort in a particular direction, the combined force breaks through barriers that would be impossible to penetrate otherwise. By being specific and garnering commitment from others in alignment with your commitment, you create that combined, active force above and beyond your own capacity.

One very important note to make is that if one or more of your supporters fails you, that doesn't give you an excuse to fail yourself. You must be reactively creative if it happens or proactively identify contingencies ahead of time.

Challenge: Make a 90-day commitment right now according to these principles. What's something you've chosen not to commit to out of fear? Now's your chance. But please don't make a commitment right now because you feel you ought to. That will nearly certainly result in failure. Only if you can own a commitment 100% right now would I suggest you make it. The opportunity is here for you to do that. If you can't own it 100%, consider what is getting in your way.

Competing Commitments

From time to time, you might discover that two or more commitments you've made are in direct competition with each other. Oftentimes, there is only the appearance of competition, and your first question should be, "How can I achieve both?" But true commitment competition does occur, and when it does, you have the unpleasant job of deciding in which you will fail and which you will achieve. I recommend you discuss the competition with any other parties involved and just be honest about the accidental conflict created. Most times, a resolution can be worked out.

Do your best to prevent this situation from occurring. Competing commitments take up a great deal of energy to resolve, and it's much better to get clarity on what is required to achieve commitments as much as possible to ensure there won't be any competition. On the flip side, if you make "foolish commitments" as described above, requirements will be less clear initially, and you may have to engage in resolving competing commitments as a result. Do not shy from creating competing commitments. It's better to over-commit than to under-commit. By over-committing, you'll quickly find and stretch the boundaries of your capacity. But don't consciously make a commitment you know you cannot complete. That really *is* foolish and unethical.

Ugly Failure

Failure finds us all. When you stick your neck so far out there, being specific, cutting off all options, publicizing your commitment, and asking others for help, failure can be particularly gut-wrenching. It's very easy to hate and abuse your Self for failing. But it is an opportunity that is potentially of equal value to the achievement of the commitment. You must forgive and accept your Self despite your failure. Remember who you really are. Remember your value is not truly determined by your performance but by your Origin's evaluation of you. Once you reestablish yourself on this strong foundation of truth, learn from your failure then move on; don't dwell on it; don't try to figure out every little detail of what went wrong. Just learn the core lessons from it and move on!

Failure doesn't deserve nearly as much attention as we give it. I've found that half the time, the cause for failure has to do with how you structure your commitment, and half the time it has to do with weakness in you and other people, though in reality, the former is merely a result of the latter. In either case, something needs to change and improve. The act of reviewing and explaining a failure is not with the intention of excusing the failure. You failed. Only forgiveness can overcome that. But failure is only negatively potent if you give it that power and fail to learn the lesson it offers.

All In, All the Time

For years, I was afraid to set audacious goals and make difficult commitments. The looming fear of failure kept me from it. I had made huge commitments and put hundreds of thousands of dollars from private investors and personal guarantors at risk and crashed and burned, taking their finances down with me. I took that personally. I didn't want to disappoint or hurt anyone else. I began to make more "reasonable" commitments, more "achievable" goals. I remember going to a seminar a couple of years after my greatest business fiasco, and the hype of the seminar excited me enough to make a crazy-huge commitment. I think it had something to do with becoming a billionaire in one year. I didn't really take into account what that would require, and I quickly discovered that it would not actually get me what I really wanted anyway. It was a desperate goal. Just in case you didn't guess, I fell rather short of it… for all intents and purposes, I fell all the way short. But within three months, I realized my poor judgment in setting that goal, and I was able to rescind it graciously.

More recently, I broke through a glass ceiling in my understanding of goals and commitments. I discovered that goals and commitments are like exercises: You set them because you want to achieve the end target, but your greatest gain is in the pursuit, in the journey. This was very important for me because it opened up the realm of possibility again, and I was able to step into the freedom of making audacious commitments and setting lofty goals, fully understanding the outcome did not reflect my worth or acceptability. Even more, it was still valuable even if I fell short because of the value I could create in the pursuit. Don't get me wrong; this isn't my way of watering down the potency of my commitments and goals. I still pursue them with all of my being. Failure simply does not have the same hold on me anymore. As with other things I've learned, I do not live in this reality perfectly, but my awareness and understanding of it makes it possible for me to respond consciously instead of battling the near-invisible subconscious.

I now look at goals entirely differently. I love goals. They are challenges I get to be creative to achieve. It's like a game or a competitive soccer match, which upon finishing, all the competitors hug, swap shirts, and feel grateful for the opportunity to compete and to give it their all to win. I care about the outcome, because my goals are attached to improving the lives of others, and that's important to me. That makes it more than just a game, but I have accepted that the most I can give in pursuing a goal is all of my strength, skill, creativity, talents, experience, etc. In short, all of my being. If I'm all in on every hand, that's what counts. No holding back; no preserving energy for the next round. All in, all the time. No excuses. I love it.

CHAPTER THIRTY TWO

LEADERS ARE INFINITELY CREATIVE

When you commit to something that is outside of your comfort zone with the intensity that is required to achieve it, you will find that you simply must be creative. When you go where you haven't gone before, you do not know what to expect, and you cannot perfectly plan for everything before getting started. If you try to plan for everything, you'll either never even get started because you've spent all your energy planning, or you'll get started with a huge delay and be surprised with obstacles you had not anticipated anyway. Keep your plan simple and clear.

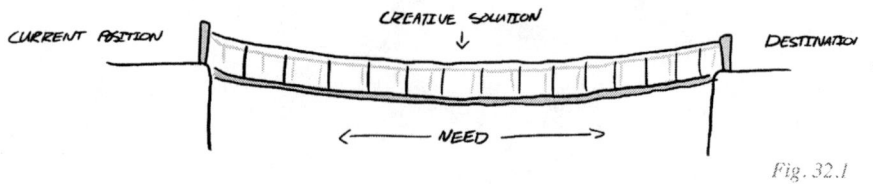

Fig. 32.1

The platitude that comes to my mind as I think about creativity is "Necessity is the mother of invention," except, in this case, I would replace "invention" with "creativity." If you make a commitment according to the principles in this book, you create a necessity for new skills, perspectives, and previously untapped strength, and that necessity generates creativity if you are clear on your current position and your committed destination, because it is the difference between those two points that represents your need, and if you are truly aware of your need and fully committed to meeting it, you cannot help but be creative *(Fig 32.1)*.

Leaders are creative by necessity. Making commitments that stretch you and require creativity to achieve is natural extension of who you are. Creativity is almost a byproduct of absolute commitment. It just happens because it must. When unexpected obstacles present themselves, you ask "How can I..." instead of "I can't" because "I can't" is no longer an option. It was one of those options you cut away when you made the commitment.

The amazing truth is that you are infinitely creative, and it is only in challenging circumstances made possible by extraordinary commitments that you test the boundless nature of your creativity. You may have to endure extreme amounts of pain and complete vacuums of comfort to overcome or circumvent obstacles that get in your way, but your creativity will show up in infinite capacity if you don't impose your own restrictions upon it. This is truly the most radical form of leadership, and it is in you to live it. This is why it is so important to choose your commitments carefully. If you're really committed to it, there's no turning back.

CHAPTER THIRTY THREE

THE RESULTS OF LEADERSHIP

The function of leadership is to allow greater and greater flows of spiritual and passionate energy to flow through a more and more effective structure to produce extraordinary results in the external world. To do this, you must grow your capacity and remove those things that are blocking and displacing the flow. Growth requires challenge and time. Removal of obstacles requires personal surgery and healing.

Growth and Planthood

LEADERS BEAR MUCH FRUIT AND MULTIPLY.

As a leader, you will necessarily experience a life that consists of tremendous, consistent growth. Just as the branch of a vine grows in its ability to allow the vine's sap to flow through it, so you can increase your capacity for the flows from your Spirit and Heart.

Growth is made possible by allowing the flow through you. The more you allow your Spirit and Heart to flow, the greater flow you will be able to handle from each in the future. A tree thickens and increases capacity the more it allows lifeblood to flow through it in a controlled, structured, productive way.

We are more like plants than you might think. Consider this: The purpose of flow in a plant is to produce and bear fruit. Fruit is produced for nourishment, enjoyment, and reproduction. In the same way, we are designed to produce fruit through our lives that builds up and brings joy to others and that plants seeds that will grow and produce more fruit, kind after kind. In short, we are designed to be fruitful and multiply. By connecting to our Origin and our Heart and opening well-structured paths for our Original Identity, Purpose, and Capacity to flow through us to the physical world, we grow and produce fruit, and the more we grow, the more fruit we are able to produce, just as a plant is able to produce more fruit the second year than the first.

Pruning: Plant Surgery

I think the grapevine is particularly representative of humanity. A vinedresser will disallow a grapevine from producing fruit the first two or three seasons to allow all of the nutritive value it draws from the soil to be committed to growing its infrastructure. If it were to grow grapes, they would be tiny and unusable anyway. In the same way, it takes time to build up a human to the point where they are able to grow fully mature fruit.

This is a great principle for business management as well. Reinvest profits for the first 2-3 years to build a strong and enduring infrastructure.

But instead of yielding our branches to our Origin, who is represented by the Vinedresser, we protect the beauty of our branches and want so badly to produce fruit earlier than is time. We want people passing by our vine to look upon it in awe at its glamorous foliage, adoring its beauty, when in reality, we are incapable of producing good fruit because all of our energy is spent maintaining the foliage. If this describes you, then you are prioritizing approval from others over Identity-driven results. You must be willing to yield and subject your image to your true Purpose and let the Vinedresser work on you, cutting away things that you are not yet ready to handle and keeping you focused on growing your capacity and infrastructure until your time comes to start bearing fruit. But be aware that even when allowed to bear fruit, every single season after a harvest, the vine is cut back to a few stubby branches.

We all have foliage in our lives. There are layers of it. It's our façade. We pour energy into maintaining it so others see us as a fruitful vine all of the time, hiding our anemic, useless fruit from view. And then we have layers and layers of disease that attach to our foliage and consume even more energy unproductively, diseases like envy, greed, resentment, bitterness, hate, complaining, and on and on and on. This stuff takes up space and chokes out good growth, displacing and crippling the Spirit and Heart flows and absorbing resources and energy that would have been used for growth and the bearing of more and better fruit.

Here's the moral of the plant story: Your life is not about

your glorification. It's not about you looking good or getting approval. Your life is about you living according to your Original Design and as a result, bearing abundant fruit. By trying to use the flow for your own glorification instead of producing fruit with it, your flow stops, or you grow useless foliage, the entangling vines weighing you down and harming other plants (people) around you.

What do you want to be: A fruitful vine or an overgrown shrubbery? And which one does your life most resemble right now?

The Functions of Fruit

Generally, "fruit" is equal to good. To bear fruit is to bring good into the world. The specific ways in which it can be made manifest are as infinite as the definition of good, so I will not try to contain them herein. Instead, I will focus on two roles that fruit plays which are in parallel with plant life.

Just like plants, leaders reproduce as a natural outpouring of who they are. They inspire and possibly train other leaders. They might duplicate business success and expand and compound quality service through those businesses to others. They might distribute ideas and produce alignment in others, which provides the opportunity for those ideas to spread through a network of aligned believers. Their success is multiplied over and over again as their fruit goes to seed and creates a positive culture in which new plants can grow. Whether it be reproducing business success, family, perspective, understanding, wisdom, skill, experience, strength, vision, and every other good thing, they are always multiplying, and their multiples get multiplied over and over again to ever-increasing levels of abundance. Enough cannot be said for the multiplicative power of leadership. Leaders beget leaders who beget leaders who beget leaders, etc. They plant seeds of opportunity wherever they go.

One final note on the value and importance of bearing fruit. It is not the goal of a leader to bear fruit. It is a natural outcome of being a leader. To pursue the bearing of fruit is to miss the point. Live according to your Original Design, and you will bear fruit as a byproduct.

I hope this comes as a very encouraging explanation of fruit. I know it is encouraging to me because for years of my life, I was striving to figure out what I ought to be doing, and never feeling like I was where I belonged. The truth that eluded me is that there are a bazillion ways to bear fruit, and by focusing on bearing fruit, I missed the point entirely. I was asking the question, "What kind of fruit should I bear?" when I should have been asking, "What kind of leader am I?"

Abundance and Scarcity

Scarcity is the belief that there is not enough to go around, that you must choose one or the other, either-or. This message is pervasive in societies around the world. The message is that we must fight to keep what we have and fight to gain more. It's a constant battle, and everyone else is fighting to get theirs, which means they're trying to take it from you. Scarcity puts us at war with everyone else. Even in our most intimate relationships, Scarcity demands that we give in order to receive and that we limit how much we give to the other person to protect our personal resources, whether it be mental, emotional, or physical energy.

Scarcity creates a transactional lifestyle of constant war, which opposes productivity and generates all manner of resentment, ill will, and bitterness between people. Scarcity demands that people embrace Egocentrism, looking out for number one first and foremost.

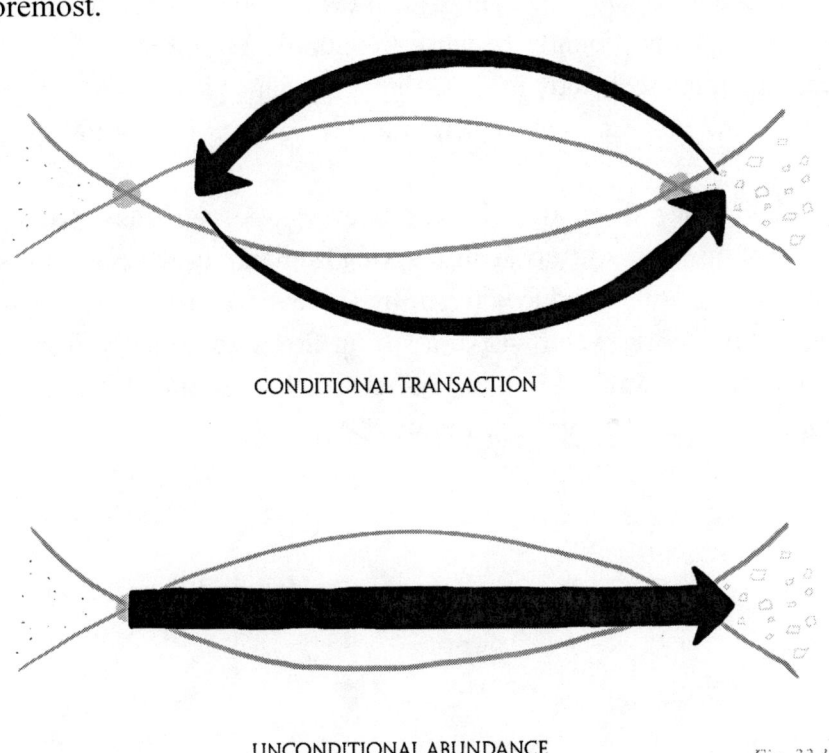

CONDITIONAL TRANSACTION

UNCONDITIONAL ABUNDANCE

Fig. 33.1

The good news is that Scarcity is only true if we are living a life defined by the world. Abundance is available through alignment with our Origin, Identity, and Purpose. Our Origin is infinite, so instead of transaction, our lives becoming a constant outpouring. It is still important to receive because it allows others to outpour effectively as well, but we do not need to receive in order to give. It's an amazing truth. We become a pass-through vessel rather than an exchange machine.

In the context of Scarcity, we give conditionally. We are bound in a transactional economy. In the context of Abundance, we can give unconditionally because the supply is limitless *(Fig 33.1)*. Many people incorrectly assume that Abundance is a position of receiving and having much, when in fact, it is a position of unlimited giving.

Springs teach us this lesson every moment they produce fresh water. You will not hear a spring demanding the clouds give it water. A spring produces fresh, life-giving water from its depths without receiving water. Like a spring flows continually from its depths, so we can never-endingly outpour life from our depths because we are living from our infinite Origin.

CHAPTER THIRTY FOUR

WHAT LEADERSHIP LOOKS LIKE

LEADERS PLAY FOR A LIVING. THEY PLAY ALL IN, ALL THE TIME.

My favorite aspect of our Original Design is that it is simple. Life is simple. I dig that. Life as a leader can be fully summed up in two parts: Being and Playing. Who I am is unchanging, so knowing who I am and living in that Identity, just being, is the ever-present ingredient in leadership according to Original Design. Playing is the action side of the equation. Playing is where we seek the better, more, and different in life. We seek to make positive changes in our lives and the lives of others. It is also where we have the opportunity to identify and respond to areas of our lives that are still in conflict with our True Identity, like turning over a new leaf and finding useless foliage beneath.

People often get this simple equation backwards. They pursue the more, better, and different, letting their performance in that pursuit define who they are. Then the pursuit ceases to be "play" and becomes "work." I don't want to work. I want to play.

The best part about play is that it is very safe, even if you play full out and take huge risks. If you are rooted in who you are, that's secure. What you do outside of that won't change who you are, so there's no risk to the essential parts of you. When you play all in all the time, you put your feet to the fire, and the only thing that'll burn up is the unproductive foliage in your life. Your Origin, Identity, Purpose are golden. Fire cannot destroy them. Falling short can cause pain to you and others, but that pain will not damage anyone's core essentials. It'll just hurt.

Play is where adventure happens. Others call it exercise or practice, and I agree it's both of those, but play includes joy by definition, and I want to live a joyful life, so I choose to play. Play is the journey, the movement in life. It's the sandbox where we get to apply our Selves, to squeeze our Selves and see what comes out. If we do not produce the results we desire, we then can review and reflect, identifying and regarding those things in us that kept us from producing the desired outcome.

As I've said before, it's not about producing the fruit. That'll happen in due course. This may be the single most important thing I write in this entire book: The value of play is in the journey, not in the end result. You do not build a sand castle for the sand castle, but for the joy in building it. If your result is an ugly sand castle, you get to knock it down and build a new one, which is also fun! If you build a beautiful, pristine sand castle, it is a pleasure to share your success with others, and others benefit from it as you share it, but the greatest value you create for yourself is in the journey of building the castle, in the playing itself.

Let me tell you something exciting. Who you really are, your Original Identity, is a master sand castle craftsman. Does that mean that you will immediately produce perfect and amazing sand castles? No. But as you live from that Identity, knowing who you are, your performance will continually come into closer alignment with your True Identity, and your capacity to produce accordingly will grow with time and play.

Play is essential to full and meaningful life. You have a choice: You can work hard or you can play hard. For life to be all play, you must get centered on who you really are, your Original Identity, and accept that. Only then can you let go of your need to perform and just play.

So be who you really are. Play all in, all the time. This is The Llama Manifesto.

APPENDIX

THE CYCLE OF GROWTH

Here's a simple guide outlining what the path to leadership looks like:

STEP 1. **Discover your Original Design. Learn the Original Truth. Reconnect to your Origin.**

Throughout this process, your Head will act as a wall of structured resistance against anything that challenges it. Soften the walls through openness. Be proactive in asking questions you've never asked in directions you've never experienced. And remain open. It's not safe, but it is necessary for growth.

This is easier said than done, obviously. If you're having trouble with this, play harder. Be more vulnerable, take more risks, set loftier goals. It is in these pressured environments that we express and release what is within us, giving us the opportunity to draw in something new and better. Find people that claim to know Original Truth and review the results in their life for evidence. Listen to everyone. Every person has something to teach you. Seek and you will find.

STEP 2. **Embrace Truth in your Head as you discover it and begin wooing your Heart into it. Yield your Will to Truth as a commitment. Do not waver from it in action.**

STEP 3.   Persistently act according to the Truth.

Your Heart will likely buck and kick in resistance against the change. Listen to your Heart, but always through the clear lens of truth. You can listen without reacting to it. As you persevere indefinitely, you will reach a point of breakthrough, at which your Heart will submit and begin to flow according to the Truth. Even after this breakthrough, your Head and Heart will still look for opportunities to return to their more comfortable patterns, so be prepared to be tested for weakness from all angles.

STEP 4.   Once you've achieved this critical alignment with your Spirit, simply flow.

Stretch your ability to guide your Heart. Guide it to greater echelons. Inspire it. And your capacity for its flow will grow, and you will bear much fruit and multiply.

This is a cycle that can revolve a million times over and beyond in your life. Undoubtedly, new opportunities to correct misalignments will present themselves along the way as there is virtually an infinite depth of layers of misalignment within you. It is the process of cutting away foliage and replacing it with Original Truth.

A CALL TO ACTION

JOIN THE LLAMA MANIFESTO

Dear Reader,

I have a vision for our generation and the next generation that will fundamentally change the global community forever. It starts with one person making the choice to step up to the plate and fully step into leadership as defined herein. As more individuals make that choice, the movement takes shape and gains traction as those few produce extraordinary results, creating space and providing an attractive environment for others to step into the same space of leadership. The movement grows all the more as more success is created from within the community of true leaders. As it reaches maturity in free, industrialized nations, it becomes the expectation rather than the exception to step into true leadership. The movement then expands globally, permeating every nation and every people, fundamentally changing our global community forever.

Can you imagine how different your life would be if the people around you stepped into this kind of leadership? What if all of your colleagues stepped into it? How would that change your organization? What if the people in your city stepped into this? How different would your city be from others? What about everyone in your state? Or nation? It's hard to fathom once the context gets that big. Through the team at Classy Llama Studios, I have had the privilege to start seeing glimpses of what it would be like. It's so awesomely different that people are nervous to join our team because they feel like they're stepping into a vastly new space like they've never experienced before. And they're right. It is vastly different.

I know the powerful impact it has had and continues to have on a microcosmic level. I can partially envision the overwhelming difference it will make on a macrocosmic level if bold people rise up into that space and are willing to be different than those around them.

So here's where it begins. It begins with me asking you to be bold and rise up into this space of extraordinary leadership. I need you. I need you to lead this manifesto with me. You and I have the opportunity to band together with others who are willing to be bold, and together, we can produce extraordinary results that flow naturally from true leadership, and by doing so, we will set the example and deliver a heralding invitation to the rest of humanity to be bold and step into this new space of leadership. And in case you're thinking I'm talking to the other readers of this book, think again. Right now, I'm talking to you. You're exactly the kind of person I need as a fellow leader in this endeavor. So please, for yourself, for your children, for humanity, commit to be bold and rise up into this space of true leadership. You have something unique that no one else can offer. I need you specifically, and so does everyone else.

Visit www.LlamaManifesto.com to find out how you can become part of and contribute to The Llama Manifesto.

With All My Being,

Kurt Theobald

ACKNOWLEDGEMENTS

This book is the product of innumerable contributions. In the end, I feel like the one who spearheaded the aggregation all of these contributions into a consolidated perspective. Specifically, I would like to thank:

Joey Southard @ Classy Llama Studios for spending countless hours producing awesome cover art, drawing amazing illustrations, and checking every detail in the formatting process. Also, for putting up with my innumerable "last-minute" changes. You were impressively flexible. I continue to be impressed by your attention and commitment to excellence in every detail. The good this book does is partly your fault.

Kristian Hansen @ Classy Llama Studios for proofreading early on in the process. Your attention to detail exceeds my own, especially in the way of grammar and punctuation. Also, if there are any mistakes in this book, it's your falte,

All the guys @ Classy Llama Studios for taking the risk with me and investing in this project. It's a blessing to have warriors standing shoulder-to-shoulder with me.

Jess, my darling wife, for being my constant encouragement that this book was important. You made as many sacrifices as I did to write this book. I am continually humbled by your commitment to me and my mission.

יהוה, for counting me worthy to commit such exciting truth to my stewardship. Your approval is enough. May this book honor you.